THE PURPOSE PLAYBOOK

SEVEN "NOT TAUGHT IN SCHOOL" LESSONS TO FIND AND FOLLOW YOUR LIFE'S PURPOSE

KYLE DENDY

WWW.KYLEDENDY.COM

The Purpose Playbook

www.KyleDendy.com

- - -

To thank you for purchasing The Purpose Playbook, please enjoy 10% OFF on all apparel from the purpose store (PurposeGangWorldwide.co) with code: P2PLAYBOOK.

To all who have ever crossed my path and said the words,
"I don't know my purpose." Your words have cut
straight to my heart and have led me to believe
that my purpose on this Earth is
to help you find yours.

CONTENTS

INTRODUCTION

THE PURPOSE PROBLEM

You have a purpose.

If death is the absence of life, millions of people die every day though their hearts still beat. They live with no direction, no aim, and certainly no plan for their life because they have no revelation of the "why" behind their being, often times because no person or institution in society, with clarity and practicality, has taught them how to make such a discovery or has encouraged them to pursue such a path. But why should life's most urgent question be neglected? Why should we train up and send out masses who soon die without discovering why they lived? Why should the mission that you alone in history have the ability to complete be aborted?

The Purpose Playbook you hold in your hands is not a mere game plan for "the good life" that many sources promise but rather is a game plan to crush your doubts, discover why you, as an individual, are here on this Earth, and teach you what you need to bet on yourself and that call that is tugging on your soul. If until today, no matter your age or background, you have meandered through life waiting for a permission slip to stop following the masses and to chase the one of a kind life and purpose you were created to live, I came to write that permission slip for you. The pages that follow are designed to expand your mind, guide you on the process of finding and following your life's purpose in a way the school system never taught you, and give you the practical twenty-first century tools you need to manifest.

Welcome to *The Purpose Playbook*,

Kyle Dendy

PART 1

DEVELOPING THE PURPOSE MINDSET

LESSON 1

FORGET WHAT YOU KNOW (SORT OF)

Think for a moment about the societal expectations generally placed upon every single one of us from the moment we are born and typically without question or challenge. In the first four to five years of your life, your parents take on the responsibility of looking out for you with the utmost care while training you in basic tasks such as speech, simple motor skills and things of the sort before eventually handing off the responsibility of your educational development to the formal education system in which you will be planted in from around age five to perhaps age eighteen if we do not include college. During this time, you will sit in straight rows and chairs, you will not speak unless spoken to, which is typically the result of a raised hand, and like the millions of other students around the world, you will be taught a curriculum created to make you a "well rounded and productive member of society." You'll spend years learning about isosceles triangles, memorizing the order of presidents, and competing for A's and GPAs because everybody knows that you can't be successful in this world if you don't graduate in the top of your class, right?

After doing this strenuous and quite stressful work for thirteen years, you'll soon discover that it could be to little avail because your future is going to come down to your ability to score well on one of two (it's important we give the kids options) standardized tests which will be taken by just about any and every student who plans to continue their education at the college level. And if you have money, you'll spend it on courses and programs that will teach you proven "guessing strategies" that will allow you to bypass the assessment of learning the test was created for in the first place and will allow you to propel yourself past the poor kid who couldn't afford the cheat codes, thus helping you attain access to the university of your choice and in turn will set you up for a life of success, so long as you don't major in art or english or something you're truly passionate about or created by God to pursue but instead choose a major that will "pay the bills," "make your parents proud," or be worth the roughly $200,000 (let's not talk about student loan debt) that you could potentially be spending on your degree with the hopes that the economy is stable enough to have a job opening for you when you graduate (because you did the work and deserve it, right?) and that the employer of your choice will be wooed by your 4.0 college GPA, your impeccable leadership skills you developed in your fraternity or sorority, and your thought provoking answer to the question, "Why are you the person for the job?" in "The coursework I completed at XYZ University was very rigorous, and though I have no actual experience, do keep in mind that I have read a great deal of industry specific case studies that have prepared me for this job and make me deserving of the salary it pays."

While many of the aspects above are obviously satirical, does it not describe the rat race and the thinking that so many young people, and even older people, in this world have as they completely disregard the idea that there could have existed a path and a purpose they were created for that would fulfill them more than any other path ever could, allowing them to look forward to waking up in the morning, be sad to leave their place of work in the afternoon, and impact the world in a way that only they could because of the unique personality and skillset that they alone in history possessed? I came to propose to you today that perhaps our desire to "go with the flow" and "pay the bills" has caused us to educate ourselves past our purpose, seek promotions in careers that distance us from our calling, and leave us to one day die without discovering why we lived.

Again, I'm not against education. I'm against being so focused on the educational and societal expectations that have been passed down unquestioned from generation to generation that the world misses the very thing you were sent here to drop off. Myles Munroe said, "Your existence is evidence that this generation needs something that is inside of you," and I came to tell you today that if you bring it forth, you can change the world, you can change your life, and you can change the life of your children's children. If perhaps you don't feel like a world changer because you don't fit the mold our society has created or because one situation or another has shattered your self worth, I am confident that if you'll read this chapter and the pages that follow with an open mind, trying to forget what you know (sort of), I'm going to pull the purpose out of you and show you the greatness that has laid dormant within you. The wisdom I share may not match your grandma's keys to success, but perhaps those keys can't open the doors you need to open in this era and the era to come.

I want you to think back for a moment to the time your self worth was most shattered or rocked. Better yet, I want you to think deeply for a moment back to the time where you stopped believing that nothing was impossible and more specifically that nothing was impossible for you. I know there was a time when you believed this because it's built into the human spirit. Children aim to be superheroes, professional athletes, and movie stars, not broke, busted, and beat up, but at one time or another either life punches them in the face with some tragic event or life altering moment, or as is common with most people, the routines, cycles, and expectations of life slowly choke out one's ability to believe that "if I shoot for the stars and miss, I might just land on the moon."

When was that moment in your life when your ability to believe was shaken? What happened? Who told you something? Who lied to you? On the lines below, I need you to be vulnerable and open with yourself about when that point was and about what happened, even if it was nothing but life's routines and expectations, for unless we identify the root of our unbelief, the fruit of it will pop up every time we try to and need to believe for something big in our life and each time we try to step into our purpose. No one has to see what's written, but the effectiveness of the exercise comes down to your ability to set aside the narrative that the past is to be "forgotten" before it is first mastered and the richness of the lessons it provided are extracted.

THE MOMENT MY BELIEF WAS SHAKEN

____

____

____

____

____

When I was in 2nd grade, I remember like it was yesterday running up to my teacher and saying, "Mrs. Huggins, I'm going to be an author one day. While I'm sure she thought it was nothing more than a cute thing for a kid to say, I can assure you that I really meant it, and as evidence of that conviction, I didn't wait for a book deal or a college degree in english. Instead, I grabbed the nearest notebook and pencil I had access to, and I started writing and writing until I had written what I advertised as my first book—*The Legend of the Great Basketball Shoe*. While, in reality, it was only a few pages long, my 2nd grade mind was convinced that I had written my first book, not because of some assigned writing project or class curriculum but because my soul said that I'm to be an author, my believing mind couldn't see why I couldn't do it right then, and my diligent hands wrote until the job was finished. While it may seem like nothing to some, what my little 2nd grade self didn't know was that I would release my first real book at age 17, my second at age 19, and that I would be writing *The Purpose Playbook* you are reading right now while still 19 years old.

While *The Legend of the Great Basketball Shoe* was nothing big at all, I believe with all my heart that my soul heard correctly those words, "I'm going to be an author" and that those childhood dreams that kids so often dream are not mere fantasies they should "grow out of," but rather are things they were born to one day "grow into." I couldn't see it back then, but my purpose was tugging and crying out and pulling on my soul, but the tragedy most people face and the reason they never become what their young believing self sought is that as they get older, they stop listening to the pull. They stop listening to the tug they once felt so strongly on their spirit. Life hits them in the mouth and the pull on their soul vanishes not because it didn't want to stay but because it ceased to receive the attention necessary to keep it alive like a beautiful plant dies if never watered.

What dream has been pulling on your soul since you were young that you dropped, buried, or put on layaway and forgot to pay for when you "got real with yourself"? If you knew you could not fail and if money was not a factor, what is it that you really want to do? When someone asks you what you want to do in life, what is the answer in the back of your mind that you decide not to share because it doesn't seem possible, so you instead share a "safe" answer that won't warrant any further questions? You get one shot at life on this Earth and because that's true, I suggest you begin to question some of the limits society has placed in your mind, and I believe that if you do this, you'll soon find that the only thing keeping you from your dreams is you.

It will take discernment and tweaking, but I believe this natural pull I described exists for the purpose of pulling you toward the purpose of your existence and reminding you of the calling on your life even when you try to forget it or even when you don't acknowledge that it's there. On the following page, then, describe the pull or the dream that you have ignored for so long, whether it be a pull from your childhood or a pull from your more recent years. Perhaps it's a desire to start a project or a desire to finish one you abandoned years ago. Whatever that pull is, be honest with yourself.

THE DREAM I HAVE SILENCED

Again, this life you live is the one shot you get on this Earth, and while it's great and can be beneficial to take advice from parents, grandparents, or guidance counselors, there will come a time when they are gone, and you will be left with your life, even if it's really nothing but the life they wanted but impressed on you. I'm not telling you to be disrespectful to anyone, but far too many people in this world miss their purpose or once in a lifetimes windows of opportunities in an effort to please people they respect, but whether you want to admit it or not, many people you respect have the agenda of keeping you safe, not the agenda of pushing you off the cliff with the belief that you can soar and not the agenda of helping you find and follow the reason you were created.

Les Brown said that "people fail in life not because they aim too high and miss but because they aim too low and hit." I have no doubt that if you decide to follow the masses, stay close to the safety net, and talk yourself out of your uncommon dreams, you possess within yourself the ability to hit all of those low goals that you have. I also have no doubt that if you aim at the low goals, you will never hit the big ones you dared not attempt to shoot for and will never experience the fulfillment that comes from doing that which you were sent to this Earth to do. "Our doubts are traitors," said Shakespeare, "and make us lose the good we oft might win by fearing to attempt." How many times in your life have you missed out on destiny because you settled for normalcy? How many times in your life have you missed out on inconceivable opportunities because you were afraid to even attempt pursuing them for one reason or another?

I actually find it very fascinating that our society is not set up to train people to find and follow their purpose because doing so would result in a society where people are in places, positions, and environments where they are most effective and engaged because they are doing something that makes them come alive and allows them to fit like a uniquely shaped puzzle piece fits in its spot. I do concede, however, that the fact that our society is set up in this way makes sense given the general, even subconscious, definition that our society gives to the word "success." Since we were young we were taught that success is good and failure is bad. If you score the most points in a game, you win, and if you don't, you lose. If you score above a certain number on a test, you pass, and if you score below that number, you fail, and the list goes on. Because we generally define success in terms of winning, money, status, security and other things of the sort, we set up institutions of society like school and family to prioritize preparing individuals to attain these things when the reality is that those are not measurements, by definition, of true success at all, and this is where the good news comes in for those who feel drawn to something they don't feel the freedom to pursue–the true definition of success was, is, and always will be "*the purpose of a thing fulfilled.*"

Did you catch that? *Success is the purpose of a thing fulfilled.* That means that the chair in your house may serve as a great place to pile up clothes after they're washed, dried, and folded, but if that chair cannot hold up a person who desires to sit on it, no matter how well it could be used for the piling up of clothes, that chair is a failure. The watch on your wrist may be beautifully encrusted with eloquent diamonds that turn heads everywhere you go, but if that watch does not have the ability to accurately tell time, that watch is either a failure or is in the act of failing until someone trained to fix it does so. This stunning truth also means, however, that even if you cannot fit the molds and expectations that everyone in society wants you to fit in such as a "good student" or a "good athlete," it does not mean that you are a failure but rather could mean that you are simply operating in a space that is outside of your purpose, thus cannot be used to measure your being a success or failure in life. Let me take this a step further.

Myles Munroe so beautifully pointed out the fact that our society speaks so often about child abuse, spouse abuse, and other types of abuse as well, all of which are terrible realities in our world, but what our society never seems to address is the most common of them all–purpose abuse. Considering the word "abuse" means "abnormal use," purpose abuse is when a person is being used for a purpose that does not match the purpose they were created for. "When purpose is unknown, abuse is inevitable," said Munroe. Think for a moment about the amount of people in this world, perhaps it's you, who know that the place they're at in life is not where they're supposed to be, but they have no idea what to do about it. That is what this book is for–helping you not just aim for something different but rather helping you first discover what that aim is so you can give that aim your life.

Until we define success as the purpose of a thing fulfilled, our society will continue to strive for success, which is a worthy pursuit, but will miss it nearly every time because the definition they hold is wrong, thus the measurement they use to judge success is inaccurate. They say, "If you're called to be a king, don't stoop to be a street sweeper, and if you're called to be a street sweeper, don't stoop to be a king." In today's society, however, most people would probably consider a king to be successful and a street sweeper to be a failure, but perhaps we have it all wrong. Dr. Martin Luther King Jr. so eloquently said that "if it falls your lot to be a street sweeper, sweep streets like Michelangelo painted pictures, sweep streets like Beethoven composed music, sweep streets like Leontyne Price sings before the Metropolitan Opera. Sweep streets like Shakespeare wrote poetry. Sweep streets so well that all the hosts of heaven and earth will have to pause and say: Here lived a great street sweeper who swept his job well. If you can't be a pine at the top of the hill, be a shrub in the valley. Be be the best little shrub on the side of the hill. Be a bush if you can't be a tree. If you can't be a highway, just be a trail. If you can't be a sun, be a star. For it isn't by size that you win or fail. Be the best of whatever you are."

You're not a failure because you can't measure

up to someone else's measurement of success. Your purpose and your aim concerns you competing to be the best you the world has ever seen, and as I mentioned in my previous book, *Godspeed*, there are no tryouts for destiny. Someone reading these words right now, I already know, is connecting with this truth on a deep level. Whoever you are, I'm begging you to hold firmly to that unique pull you feel because it's not about you but about every person whose life will be impacted because you had the guts to bet on yourself and the call of God on your life. Would you rather be a cheap copy of something great or a one of a kind masterpiece that no one in eternity can ever replicate?

As, in your life, you begin to shoot for this word called "success," I need you to understand that it's not measured in terms of money, status, fame, or anything of the sort. If you become rich or famous in your life, then more power to you, but success is measured not by those things but by your doing what you were born to do.

Success could look like the elementary school teacher who discovers her purpose to teach and understands the residual impact she will have on the lives of the kids she raises up, and so she raises up kids who learn to love themselves, believe in themselves, and to do the same for those around them. Success could look like the older lady who works in a middle cafeteria, not because she couldn't be doing something else but because she feels called to that post and is living a life worthy of the calling she has received. Success could look like the mother who on New Year's Day 2003 walks into her house with her two children as they unexpectedly see her husband and their father just after he committed suicide, and she needs to be sad, she needs to be down, she needs to mourn, and she deserves the ability to do so but looks over and sees two twin five year old kids looking up in her eyes and needing her to be strong and so she was strong, as was the case with my mother, my twin sister, and myself.

Again, if your journey leads you to money, status, or fame, there is nothing inherently wrong with that and much good can come from those platforms or positions of influence, but too many gurus, self help books, and seminars, are geared toward making that your aim and in turn are propelling you right past your purpose, and as a result, you are left in a rat race that has you hustling to be good enough instead of understanding that you are enough and hustling from that place of wholeness. When you are whole before you hustle, the world can't distract you from the true mission and calling you were born to fulfill. Let prosperity catch you on an intersection with Purpose Road.

Now that we have redefined success with a more accurate description that will carry you throughout this Purpose Playbook process, I would like to diagram what it takes to reach this place of real success–purpose fulfilled. Remember, this is not a playbook for "Seven Steps to Worldly Success." This is a playbook to discover your purpose so you can fulfill that purpose and do the very thing you were created to do, shaped to do, and that will fulfill you. Take a moment to look over the diagram below.

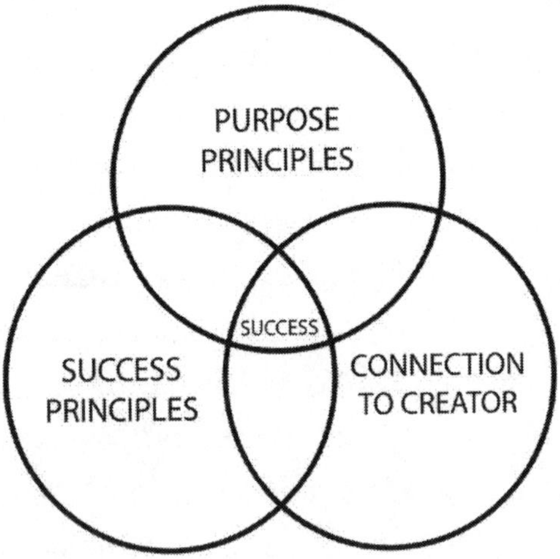

While much of this book will focus on the "purpose principles" circle, many miss true success because they have one or two, but rarely three, of these circles satisfied in their life. Think about all of the times you've heard about a celebrity or millionaire who had more money than they could ever imagine but ended up taking their life. While it varies from person to person, perhaps they had the success principles down–they understood the power of the mind, the science of money, the principles outlined in books like Napoleon Hill's *Think and Grow Rich*, etc. but though they had "the keys to success" as the world would put it, the ability to gain the world wasn't enough to satisfy their soul. Let's be even more generous and say that this person understood the purpose principles as well and, on one dimension or another, was operating in the arena of life they were created for. Still, without a connection to their creator, the most important element of the purpose discovery process, the soul of that person will still be longing for something more and will still feel a void of emptiness that perhaps they mask with busyness in order to create the external appearance that everything internal is intact. Why? Because when a branch begins to believe that it is on its own accord that it is producing fruit and separates itself from the vine, that branch dies.

The optimal position, then, to do everything you were created to do and to live a life in which you are walking in your purpose with the void in your soul filled, is to learn and apply the purpose principles to discover why you are here while also learning and applying the success principles to align yourself with laws as real as gravity while day by day connecting to and moving closer to God your creator. Just like the manufacturer of the car you drive or the phone you have, only the creator of a person or thing knows precisely that creation's true purpose, true limits, and special features hidden to the naked eye. God knows you more than you know yourself, and in relationship with him, he will guide you through the process of your production, showing you how you were made and showing you what you were made for.

It is also important, however, that a person not expect their connection to their creator to automatically do the work of fulfilling the purpose their creator gave them. God will guide you where you are to go, provide provision for the vision he gives, and bring confirmation along the way, but he will not grab you by the feet and make you walk, he will not make you get out of bed when the alarm clock goes off, and he will not bless your apathy. When you arrive at the harmony of each of the three circles diagramed, however, success–the fulfillment of your purpose–is on its way.

In our society's current dynamic, a billion dollar self help industry exists to fulfill one's desire to learn success principles and churches on every corner aim to strengthen one's connection to their creator. While either of those two groups may touch on purpose, both too often leave a person asking, "What's next? I read the books and learned the processes to turn dreams into realities, but what's next?" Or "I surrendered my life to God and want to glorify him with the gifts and the call he gave me, but what does that look like on a practical level (this is key) in my life as a student, single mother, working individual, or just as a human being, period? You told me that my purpose is to glorify God, but you didn't tell me how to do that when the church service is over and the alarm clock goes off on Monday morning."

The purpose of this book and the pages that follow is to help you, on the most practical level possible, answer the question, "What's next?" And more specifically, "What is next for *your* life? What has God created you to do that you haven't discovered yet? And how do you make that happen in this unique era in history?" Read the following chapters with diligence as you begin this practical journey of purpose discovery, and remember, if you're going to find your life's purpose, you must forget what you know (sort of).

LESSON 2

KILL THE SIX ASSASSINS

"The wealthiest places in the world are not the gold mines of South America or the oil fields of Iraq or Iran," said Myles Munroe. "They're not the diamond mines of South Africa or the banks of the world. The wealthiest place on the planet is just down the road. It is the cemetery. There lie buried companies that were never started, inventions that were never made, bestselling books that were never written and masterpieces that were never painted. In the cemetery is buried the greatest treasure of untapped potential. There is a treasure within you that must come out. It is your potential. Don't go to the grave with your treasure still within you." While there exist many more, this chapter will overview and teach you how, on a practical level, to defeat six of the most powerful assassins of the unique purpose you were created for–assassins whose sole purpose is to cause you to die without ever discovering why you lived and to settle for an "okay" life which you may be accustomed to but is, in fact, below your potential and life's call.

If you're like most people in this world, you already know that ridding yourself of even just one of these six assassins would cause your life to look much different than it looks right now, and what's interesting is that this is true for most "success principles" you'll ever hear about–everyone knows what they are, everyone knows what they should do, but their life never changes because they simply won't do it. The "secrets to success" have been mined, tested, proven, and shared for thousands of years, but people still don't use them because their hope for a shortcut makes them believe that success can be found without discipline, work, time management, planning, persistence, and every other basic principle they've heard about all their life.

It's the reason a person starts a new diet or workout plan every other month because the last one "wasn't the one for them," when in reality they've just never stuck with something long enough to see results. Want to know a secret? Want to know which diet and which workout plan is going to get you the results you're looking for even though the market is saturated with gurus telling you to try theirs? It's simple really. The greatest diet and the greatest workout plan is… wait for it… the one you stick with. It's the one you focus on with discipline and persistence until the results are attained. Exercise works. Eating healthy works. It's proven by science and has worked for millions. You're not an exception. You just quit every time you don't get the instant gratification this culture has grown you accustomed to.

The reason I tell you this is because, again, the same is true with all of the basic, boring, mundane success principles you've heard of all your life. They work, but only if you stick with them. If you don't get the result you seek, the principles have not failed but rather you have failed at some point in time to see them through, often times because you lack persistence or patience. It's time to get rid of the "those people are exceptions" mindset and step into your destiny. Yes, some people seem to be dealt easier hands than others, but you have in your hands the cards you were dealt, and just like every card game has different rules and objectives, when you begin to understand that your individual purpose on this Earth is not like anyone else's in eternity, you realize that you can succeed with the cards in your hand because they are the exact cards you need for the purpose you have.

As you read about each assassin, study it carefully like a professional sports team would study their opponent before a big game. Study its strengths, its weaknesses, and your personal susceptibility to fall under the trap of each one. Know when it stalks, and know when it strikes. Know how to kill it before it kills you, and as soon as you learn about each one, immediately begin putting into action your plan of attack.

ASSASSIN 1: PROCRASTINATION

This first silent assassin will choke the life out of every dream, aspiration, and responsibility you have if you don't kill it and kill it fast. It's the persuasive liar that whispers in your ear that binge watching eight seasons of a show on Netflix is a better option than taking care of the more important and immediate responsibilities in your life that could include, but are not limited to, your education, occupation, family, or even mundane, but important, day to day tasks like taking out the trash, writing that paper, maintaining your hygiene, or going to sleep at a healthy time. Procrastination is a narrative which becomes a mindset that tells you spending hours each and every day living vicariously through the lives of others on social media will somehow cause your own goals to get accomplished.

If you don't learn how to stop procrastinating, you can forget about ever being successful, you can forget about ever fulfilling your purpose, and you can forget about ever completing things of real value during your time here on this Earth. I'm not trying to tell you that it's not a hard habit to break but only that you need to make up your mind and choose between Netflix marathons or arriving at your purpose, destiny, and even the smaller goals you have. Why? Because you can't have your cake and eat it too.

Stop lying to yourself and everyone else saying you want something in your life to change when you waste time every day doing the same mindless things that progress you nowhere closer to the goals you say you have. I'm not against watching Netflix, playing video games, or having a good time with the people in your life, but each of us has been allotted only 24 hours in a day. Each of us have 86,400 seconds each day to do everything we're going to do, say everything we're going to say, and go everywhere we're going to go, so stop saying you don't have time to do the important things if an audit of your life would expose your lies.

If you haven't caught on by now, I'm playing no games with this book, and I'm not writing to tell you,

"you're doing great" if you're not. I'm writing to crush your excuses, kill your assassins, and pull you toward the purpose you were created for even if I have to drag you there. Why? Because there are people in this world who are depending on what you are called to do. This is no time to sing "Kumbayah" or play patty cake at the neighborhood block party. Look around the world. Look around your country. Look around your city. Look at yourself. I'm writing this book about purpose because the world needs yours, and this is good news for you because this means that if you find your purpose, you don't have compete with the next person who graduated with the same GPA as you did, placing your hopes in the likelihood that your hiring employer doesn't catch the typo in your resume. Purpose is your key to the doors of your success.

As it often times falls into one of two simple categories, I want to make very clear the reason for your procrastination and to provide you with a step by step strategy to kill it. The reason you procrastinate on the individual tasks of your day is, quite simply, that those tasks don't mean enough to you, and the reason you procrastinate in general, just going through the motions in life, is that you have nothing you're aiming at, nothing you're moving toward, and no sense of purpose for your life.

I know that your procrastination as it pertains to the individual tasks of your day is the result of those tasks not meaning enough to you because if I had a million dollars waiting for you if you finished your seven page research paper this week instead of next week, you would get it done today and say, "Where's my money?" If you found out that your employer was going to give you the promotion of your dreams at work the next day if you simply showed up on time, you would lay your clothes out the night before, wake up on the first alarm you set, and show up early with a smile on your face. Why is this true? Because you interpret the rewards of the actions to be valuable enough for you to get them done quickly and with excellence. You don't procrastinate in these situations because the tasks mean enough to you.

With that in mind, I understand that often times in your life you find a task before you that has no major reward but needs to get done. While killing the procrastination of these tasks can be found in a number of solutions based on the varying scenarios, I will describe three:

1. The Social Media Procrastination

If you have a tendency to scroll through the ever-updating social media apps on your phone when you should be completing some task like work or school, get out an old fashioned piece of notebook paper or an index card and make a numbered list, in order of priority, of the assignments you need to complete that particular day. Order this list with the most important tasks coming first, then DELETE the social media apps from your phone until you complete the assignments (Note: They'll still be available to download again when you finish. Don't panic.).

This last part is important because of the barrier to entry you create around the distraction, social media, by deleting it instead of just closing it. If you close it only, you'll likely find yourself picking up your phone and opening Instagram or Facebook without even thinking, but if you delete it, there exists a whole process that you would have to consciously overtake to allow the distraction back in. This is what much of success comes down to–moving negative habits from the subconscious mind to the conscious mind and moving positive, beneficial habits from the conscious mind to the subconscious mind.

As Earl Nightingale puts it, however, "The problem is that our mind comes as standard equipment at birth. It's free. And things that are given to us for nothing, we place little value on.

Things that we pay money for, we value. The paradox is that exactly the reverse is true. Everything that's really worthwhile in life came to us free: our minds, our souls, our bodies, our hopes, our dreams, our ambitions, our intelligence, our love of family and children and friends and country. All these priceless possessions are free. But the things that cost us money are actually very cheap and can be replaced at any time. A good man can be completely wiped out and make another fortune. He can do that several times. Even if our home burns down, we can rebuild it. But the things we got for nothing, we can never replace."

Think on this for a moment. This is why the fulfillment of your life's purpose, no matter how big, can be achieved. Perhaps you don't need more money, resources, or even time. Perhaps you just need to use the mind that was freely given to you. Individuals, no less human than you, used their minds to invent flying machines in bicycle shops and scribe revolutionary writings from prisons around the world. They weren't born "exceptions." They used their minds to become them.

2. The "This Task is So Big" Procrastination

If you are like many in this world, you probably have

a tendency to procrastinate when the task before you seems so large that even thinking about it brings you great stress or anxiety. If this is you, I want you to answer a question that will seem rather odd at first glance: how do you eat an elephant? How do you eat something so big and so monstrous that you don't know where to start? The answer is simple: You eat an elephant… one bite at a time, and the same is true for taking control of and completing the big, monstrous tasks that you come across in your daily lives. If you look at the whole project, you'll never have the courage to start, but if you break the project down into individual tasks and break the tasks down into individual steps, you'll see that the biggest accomplishments are often found in the smallest of tasks executed upon day by day for extended periods of time.

If you have a 10 page report to write and you wait until the night before it's due to begin writing, of course it will seem big, but if you break it down into a page a day, the big task becomes small. If you set a goal of losing 50 pounds and every time you go to the gym or get on the scale, the number 50 is on your mind, the goal will seem distant for a large period of time and may discourage you, but if you first understand that losing 50 pounds starts with losing five pounds and that losing five pounds starts with losing one pound and even that losing one pound starts with losing half a pound, you begin to celebrate the small victories and to realize that the big ones are nothing but a culmination of the small. You can kill this type of procrastination by breaking big projects down into smaller tasks, by celebrating small wins on the journey, and most importantly, by making a decision to start. Every action and every step on the journey to getting where you want to go begins with a decision.

3. The "Low Self Confidence" Procrastination

Another common reason that we procrastinate is that we have little confidence in ourselves as it relates to our ability to be successful at whatever the present task is. It's the reason a guy who for months has wanted to speak to a girl he sees all the time continues to put it off saying, "I'll wait for a better opportunity," when in reality he simply doesn't have the confidence to speak. It's the reason a gifted working individual who knows that they are worth more than they are being paid continues to put off bringing it up to their boss because they don't have the confidence to ask for a raise or the confidence to leave and take their skills elsewhere, and so they settle in a job they could do blindfolded because of a mind that lacks confidence.

What areas of your life have you allowed low self confidence to cause you to procrastinate doing what you know you ought to do? One of the first steps you ought to take to overcome this limitation is to take captive every thought and every narrative running in your mind that is telling you "what is probably going to happen." Next, repeat to yourself until you believe it that your value is not at all tied to someone else's ability to see it. The girl you've been wanting to talk to probably wouldn't think twice about having a conversation with you, but even if she told you to your face to "get away," that's her problem, not yours. If you know that you are providing more value in the form of a service to some organization and are not being rewarded appropriately, perhaps your boss will hear you out and still turn down your request, but that is not a determinant of your personal value or even of the value you are providing to the company but only a determinant of one person or organization's ability to see it. Remember, the quickest way for your request to be rejected is for your request to never be proposed at all. As I will write on later in this book, there comes a time when you must be willing to bet on yourself, and if you know what you've got, what you've got will be enough.

The above are three examples of ways you can work to kill procrastination as it pertains to specific tasks or situations you have encountered or likely will encounter in your life, but I also understand that for the vast majority of people, your biggest problem is that procrastination for you is a way of life that taps into everything. You don't just procrastinate about certain tasks, you have a procrastination mindset that causes you, in life, to just go through the motions every single day. Maybe you're in college, maybe you're a working adult, or maybe you're retired, but you wake up every day with no aim in mind, you go to bed each night with nothing more you wish you had time to work on, and when people ask you what you're up to in life, your response is, "I'm just going with the flow" every single time.

This may hands down be the most dangerous, and dare I say lethal, of all procrastination mindsets because the flow is like a lazy river in which you go around so many times that you forget how long you've been in it, and you don't want to leave because you've found comfort in the rhythm. There is only one way to kill this virus and that is to get a clear vision of something to aim for, something to move toward, or something to live for. This clear vision I am referring to is your purpose. Because you're not moving toward anything, "going with the flow" and procrastinating as a way of life doesn't conflict with anything, but when you get a clear picture of your aim, when you get a clear picture of your purpose, there no longer exists time to procrastinate because you're busy chipping away at a vision day by day.

I can't tell you exactly what this vision is for you, but I can tell you that if you don't find it, procrastination will naturally sneak in and kill any hope of you succeeding in life as it relates to our definition of success as "purpose fulfilled" because going with the flow and living a "whatever happens happens" life with the hopes that you one day end up "somewhere good" simply won't work. No one hits a bullseye if they have no aim at all. There's a bullseye, a mark, a target, a purpose for your life that you can only hit if you aim for it. As I'll talk about more in the pages ahead, starting your pursuit toward your purpose is not about seeing the whole journey ahead of time but about running toward the call on your life as soon as you get a glimpse of it and about placing yourself in position for a life of purpose in which you are doing what you were created to do.

ASSASSIN 2: LIMITING BELIEFS

This next assassin has possibly killed more dreams

and prevented the fulfillment of more purposes than any of the over five combined because the call on a person's life is always bigger than where they are at their present time, and it is nearly impossible to reach a place that one does not know exists. If a person is limited in their understanding of what is possible in this world and for their life, they can never aim at the bullseye called their purpose and at the very best will merely hit some mark on the target as a whole. For this reason, we must kill the assassin of limiting beliefs before these beliefs kill our hope of finding, following, and fulfilling our life's purpose in the time we have before our life comes to an end.

I remember as a little kid one of my favorite things to do was to walk to the park just outside of my neighborhood and spend as much time as was given to me running around, swinging on the monkey bars, and just being a kid. On one trip in particular, however, this was anything but the experience I had. Like any other day, I walked to the park with my mother and began walking up the steps of the playground, but this time I was greeted by the voice of another little kid who stopped me, saying, "You can't come up here because you have black skin." When he said these words, I felt frozen, for it was the first negative experience I had ever had concerning the color of my skin. It was the first time someone had, to my face, aimed to make me feel inferior because my skin was darker than theirs.

In my situation, the natural response, and the response that many choose, was one of allowing the opinions and words of this other person to limit my thinking about my value and about my potential. If I didn't have a mother who immediately stepped into the situation, called out the boy for his words, and also affirmed me of my value thus cutting that limiting belief at the root, perhaps that seed would have grown into something bigger. Too many people have insecurities that spawned not from their own thinking but from the ignorant thoughts and opinions of others and because these insecurities were not cut short when they came up, these people are kept from stepping into much of the greatness and achievement that lies within them. Without even recognizing it, they find themselves settling for "okay" left and right until they've sprinkled their "*okay*" dust on every single thing that God is trying to do in their life.

The reason many fall into this trap of settling for an "okay" level in life is that the experiences they've had and the achievement or lack thereof that they have seen is simply all they know. Until a person knows that more is possible, they will always settle for less, and for this reason exposure is one of your greatest weapons in your fight against the assassin of limiting beliefs. Just because your mother or your father never went to school, doesn't mean that's the limit for you. Just because no one "from where you're from" has started a business, doesn't mean that's the limit for you. Just because all you know is "okay" does not mean that you haven't been created, crafted, and called for extraordinary. In order to reach these new heights of achievement, however, you must expose yourself to the land of "more" and distance yourself from the land of "less."

Perhaps this looks like cutting off people who are always and only bringing negative energy, sarcasm, and complaints into your space. Perhaps this looks like unfollowing on Instagram or unfriending on Facebook the people (you know exactly who I'm talking about) that are always talking about how bad the world is, complaining about how bad their life is, and posting content that does nothing but create division. These people have to go if you are going to find, follow, and fulfill your life's purpose because doing so requires a level of thinking that these people will always try to pull you down from. Instead of filling your mind with the thoughts and opinions of the aforementioned individuals, find and follow people who think on the level of your future not your past or even your present. Find and follow individuals who have no time for gossip and complaining because they are walking in their own purpose, reaching their own goals, and are generous enough to share their journey with you or with the public.

By making phone calls, sending texts messages, or connecting online, find mentors who can see in you traits and characteristics you can't see in yourself or at the very least will allow you to ask them questions about their journey which will inevitably expose you to ideas and possibilities you had not previously conceived and therefore could not previously achieve. In doing so, you'll quickly discover that these individuals will push you toward your destiny by pulling the purpose out of you.

It's also important that you read books from and about people who are living lives of meaning and purpose and are dropping clues about how you can do the same especially if their route or vision is similar to yours. Watch videos online from leaders, both motivational and spiritual, who are teaching lessons and keys that will be necessary for you to unlock certain doors in your life. In this twenty-first century, resources are all around us to the extent that we have no excuse to have no exposure to what is possible.

Now, keep in mind that in the digital age we live in, many can and will pose like they've got their ducks in a row but really are fake when it comes down to it. Don't trust a person just because they have "followers" and don't neglect a person simply because they don't. Often times the greatest gems will be found in the most mundane looking vessels. One meeting, one lunch, one encounter with one ordinary person may be all it takes to push you from the land of ordinary to the land of extraordinary. Remember, your purpose is something which is carried out on a journey over the course of time and when you one day come to the end of that journey, you'll see that the big achievements and mountaintop moments never would have happened without the presence of small dates with destiny we commonly called "coincidence" but in actuality were divine.

It's time to step out of the "failure" mentality that has controlled your every decision for so long. You were not put on this Earth to fail but to succeed by fulfilling a purpose in a specified amount of time which I know is enough for you because your creator gave or is giving you everything you need, including the time, to do so. Everything you could possibly need is at your fingertips or is closer than you think, but if you don't expand your vision, I can promise you one thing–you will never find and follow your purpose. Yes, it's bigger than your current situation, but it's not your responsibility to do what's not possible. You take care of what is possible with what is in your hand right now, and if you are faithful with that, God will take care of the rest and take you from level to level and from your present to your purpose.

I don't know what words someone spoke to you eight years ago that you are convinced are the reason you're not where you want to be, but I'm writing this to tell you that what they said about you does not have to become your reality. It doesn't matter how many negative words someone speaks over your life or even how many positive words someone speaks over your life. All that matters is the words that you believe and the conversation, whether limited or expanded, that is happening in your mind when you think about your purpose–not knowing exactly what it is but simply knowing that it's bigger than where you are right now and even if you don't know where you're going, you simply know that you can't stay where you are.

Purpose is never found in the nest of comfort and familiarity but rather inside the bird that jumps from the nest for the first time and thinks to itself, "I'm going to fly because I have no other options." You were born for greatness and though there is a process that occurs on your journey to your prime and the achievements that follow, there is still much to learn, much to love, and much fulfillment to be had on this long street called Purpose Road. Choke the limiting beliefs when they arise and tell yourself every day, "Not only *can* I fly…but I was born to."

What limiting beliefs about yourself, about your potential, or about your purpose have stopped you from flying and have caused you to convince yourself that the nest of "okay" isn't all that bad and that the nest, or environment, you were born in is one that you might as well stay in? What beliefs appeared when someone covered you with negative words that you let stick? Use the lines below to be vulnerable with yourself, own each belief, and dispel each of them by coming to a conclusion about the truth and rehearsing that conclusion until it becomes natural in the recital of life.

MY TOP THREE LIMITING BELIEFS ABOUT MYSELF

1. ________________________________
2. ________________________________
3. ________________________________

ASSASSIN 3: ASSOCIATION

If you've ever heard the wise old saying, "You become like the five people you spend the most time with," you probably understand the direction that this section of the chapter is going to go. The assassin of association lurks in the shadows of your everyday life and everyday relationships and has the ability to exponentially increase or decrease the likelihood that you will succeed in life by arriving at the places you were created to arrive at and by doing the things you were created to do in the time you were allotted on this Earth. For this reason, it is important that you find and surround yourself with people who are going in the same direction as you and, as someone once advised me, can hop on the train without asking you to slow it down. Destiny has a clock and time waits for no man. Tomorrow is not guaranteed and keeping the wrong company will guarantee that you spoil the time you have today. It's time to take inventory of your dream team and make cuts where necessary.

I would like you to take a moment to think about the five closest people in your life. What do they look like? What do they sound like? How do they act? Who are the people you spend the most time with? Who are the people that know you the best? Who are the people who are in your inner circle? If all five are broke, I'm guessing you're the sixth. If all five party their weekends away, I'm guessing you're the sixth. If all five are out of shape and unhealthy, I don't even have to look at you to make an educated guess that you are out of shape and unhealthy as well. Why? Because "you become like the five people you spend the most time with," and if this is true in the negative–that lazy, unsuccessful, unmotivated friends will cause you to become the same–the reverse must also be true in the positive. It must also be true that if you surround yourself with the people of your purpose not the people of your past, you too will start to look like, sound like, act like, and become like those people. Why? Because "the mind of man, once stretched by a new idea or experience, never returns back to its original dimensions" (Oliver Wendell Holmes). When you rub shoulders with greatness, greatness begins to rub off on you, and it's not that you "forgot where you came from" but rather that you remember where you came from and know that you don't want to go back.

As I mentioned earlier, I told my teacher in second grade that I was going to be an author, and so I did it, but I wonder what would have happened if she had shot down my dream and told me that I would never reach that goal. In that same second grade year, as I sat in a restaurant in Dallas, TX and listened to my mother talk about this foreign concept called "entrepreneurship," I got a pen and a napkin and sketched the business plan for my first business–

Kyle's Shoe Shining Company–and would go around the neighborhood with business cards, clients, and grit, but I wonder what would have happened if my mother, who was in my inner circle, had mentioned entrepreneurship but had shot down my aspirations to start so young.

When I was 17, I released my first official book and began traveling as a speaker and have now toured the United States with this message of purpose, have written multiple books, have been on television, have produced content viewed by millions of people worldwide, and have done so much more, but I wonder what would have happened if I had surrounded myself, like most do, with people who's sarcasm crippled my dreams and ultimately my destiny when they were merely ideas. Be careful sharing big dreams with small minded people, and be even more careful sharing big dreams with sarcastic people because while it seems to be a joking matter to them, those words they speak are planted in your mind as seeds, and it's in those midnight hours as you toss and turn in bed thinking about and replaying those words, that you are actually watering those seeds, sometimes with tears, thus giving them the power to grow into a plant called the assassin of association. Who are you associating with?

The problem for many is that some of our

strongest associations are not those we chose but rather are those that were ushered into our lives in the form of family, classmates, or childhood friends. There was a time when we did life on their level–living like they live, talking like they talk, and dreaming like they dream–but their came a time when we caught a glimpse of our destiny that did not match that present situation, leaving us caught in the crossfire of a battle between a mind that says, "There's more out there for me" and a geographic reality that says, "But this is where I am." What do you do when you're caught in the space between your present and your future? What do you do when the vision for your life you saw doesn't match the vision for your life that those around you project into your mind day by day because they can't see anything bigger for themselves or for you? What do you do when you want to jump toward that dream you have but know that doing so will lead to criticism, sarcasm, and a "who do you think you are?" speech that will be locked in to shoot down your dream like heat seeking missiles in a war?

The first thing you must do when you find yourself in this dilemma is understand that you are not obligated to give an account of your future to everyone who asks or to everyone around you. Your life's vision and life's purpose will be revealed to you, not to them, so you can't expect everyone to see what you see if they never received the vision you were given. Besides, if you give a PowerPoint presentation of your dreams to everyone in your present environment, you are going to waste the valuable emotional and mental energy that you will need to invest into those dreams to make them happen.

Some people will come to you and outright tell you that you're crazy and that you can't do it while others will come to you with honest intentions trying to "speak some sense into you" because they're a "seasoned adult" and "used to think big too" before reality kicked in and bills had to be paid. Both of these groups will drain you as you listen to the same spiel worded a hundred different ways, but trust me when I tell you that if you hold out on sharing your vision until the right few visionaries cross your path, you will be electrified with a burst of emotional fuel which will be necessary for your vision to be reached, and some of these few visionaries will become friends, or even inner circle brother or sisters, who will push you to your purpose when you're going too slow and will pull you toward your destiny when you're ready to give up. If all you find is five of these people to be a part of your inner circle in replace of the negative, mentally-draining people that occupied those spots before, you have more than enough weaponry to kill the assassin of association and will even go so far as to turn that assassin into an asset.

Take a moment now to look over the following six signs of a toxic inner circle, and prepare to fire from your inner circle team those who match the following red flags:

1. People you have to "mentally prepare" to speak to about your aspirations because they always have something to say and it's seldom positive or those you don't feel comfortable talking to about your aspirations at all for similar reasons.
2. People who are sarcastic about everything and have a special ability to find the negative in every positive, even in a humorous way.
3. People who are unmotivated and have no goals, leading them to aim at and move toward nothing in life. Whether verbally or in a passive aggressive way, these people attempt to get you to do the same.
4. People who are always gossiping to you or around you about everyone and everybody. If they're talking about others when you're around, they're talking about you when you're not.
5. People who always seem to have a jealous chip on

their shoulder. These people are especially dangerous because they may be able to match your charisma and visionary mentality but only with the intent to steal from or destroy your creative vision.

6. People who can never keep their mouth shut. The last thing you need is to have your well thought out idea or vision plastered across social media while it's still in the building phase.

How many of these six signs matched the characteristics of those in your inner circle? If a person is *progressively* and *intentionally* working to fix the negative tendencies they have, that's one situation, but if a person shows no sign of change or a desire to change, CUT THEM OFF today. If you don't, they'll cut you off from the path to your purpose with the assassin of association.

ASSASSIN 4: INSECURITY

While the chances are high that I will never have the opportunity to meet you face to face, I am sure of this–that if you are a human being walking this Earth, in some form or fashion you deal with insecurity. Perhaps you feel that you are too tall or too short, too light or too dark, too fat or too skinny, too shy or too outgoing. All of us have insecurities that we try to cope with every day as we navigate a world where we feel constantly compared to, and often times compare ourselves to, those other insecure individuals around us. We all deal with insecurity, but the fact that the problem is universal does not mean that it is not vital we confront it on our own individual journey toward the discovery and fulfillment of our purpose before it paralyzes us in our tracks and stops us from ever manifesting said purpose.

To better understand the insecurities you deal with and more specifically to better understand why you deal with these insecurities in the first place, I want to paint for you a picture described by Earl Nightingale in which we have before us a beautiful garden, and for the sake of this example, let's say that this was a good garden with fertile soil, thus possessing the nutrients needed for whatever you decided to plant therein. Now, suppose you have in your hand two seeds–one of corn and one of nightshade, a deadly poison. Let's say, then, that you bury in the ground both of these seeds, you cover them with dirt, you water them on a regular basis, and you take care of the land like you're supposed to. If you do this, the garden will "return poison in just as wonderful abundance as it will corn." Why? Because the garden never cared what you decided to plant but, by nature, it would return whatsoever you planted and watered.

In the same way, the garden described above represents your mind and the seeds, whether corn or deadly nightshade, represent the thoughts and beliefs that were planted in your mind, even subconsciously, from the time you were born until now. Some of them were good seeds and some of them were poisonous seeds. It is these poisonous seeds, then, that five, ten, twenty, even forty years later are still manifesting themselves in your mind and in your life as insecurity because you watered them for so many years without even knowing it.

With all of this being said, the question then remains, what do we do about it? How do we kill our insecurities? How do we overcome the feeling of not being good enough? How do we overcome the feeling of not being attractive enough? How do we change the mindsets that we know are detrimental to our progress and to our purpose but seem too big to conquer? While the answer is by no means simple and while these negative seeds you have been watering for years will not be eliminated overnight, there are five practical steps I can offer for those who have had enough of the insecurities that have robbed them of so much joy in life and are ready to step into their purpose with confidence. The five steps I have to offer will require courage, but if you are willing to exercise them, they will change your life and will help you kill the assassin of insecurity.

1. Identify Your Insecurities by Name

One of the most underrated abilities in this era in history is self-awareness, or the ability to understand and identify your individual characteristics, feelings, and mental forces. As powerful as this skill is, most people are very poor at it. As a result, failure becomes a way of life in many areas of their life because every time they try something and fail, they move on to something else without ever identifying the cause of their failure and thus being able to correct it for the future. It's like getting sick and never getting a proper diagnosis. You continually take medicine or try solutions that would work for a certain problem, but won't solve the problem you have. You don't know that, however, because you haven't identified the problem in the first place. If we are going to kill your insecurities, we must identify them like a brain surgeon who must operate with precision.

What I want you to do, then, is to use the lines below to identify, by name, the top three insecurities you know haunt you each day. As mentioned before, no one has to see this but you, but the exercise will only work if honesty is prioritized. The only way we can kill an insecurity is by first identifying it.

MY TOP THREE INSECURITIES

1. ______________________________
2. ______________________________
3. ______________________________

Now that you have identified three of your top insecurities, I want you to think about each one of them independently and ask yourself, first, "In what specific situations or types of situations does this insecurity arise?" For example, perhaps the first insecurity you listed is that you always feel like people are judging you or like eyes are always on you in a negative way. If this is the case, perhaps the situation which triggers this insecurity is walking through the hallways in your school or walking through the office at your place of work. Perhaps this insecurity causes you to look at the floor as you walk instead of keeping your head up and walking with confidence.

The reason I want you to identify what triggers this particular insecurity is so that the next time it happens, you will be aware of the insecurity in your conscious mind, which leads to the second step: look at the insecurity you listed from an objective point of view. By this I mean that as human beings, we have a subconscious tendency to read into things, to confirm biases we already have, and to assume the worst. Looking at the example above from an objective point of view would mean recognizing that every single person you think is judging you, in reality, has too many things on their own mind to waste time thinking about you all the time.

Studies say that a person has 50,000-70,000 thoughts per day. If you mix that with their own fears, anxieties, worries, places to be, and things to do, you'll realize that most of the time you think people are judging you, they probably don't even notice you, and in the off chance they are judging you, let that be their problem not yours.

Most of the people you're worried about are people who you'll either never see again or whose opinions have no bearing on your future. Identify which situations trigger each of the insecurities you listed, and next time that trigger goes off, analyze the situation and the insecurity from an objective perspective, and I believe you'll begin to notice that the insecurity may be more irrational than you thought and this new perspective will help you kill your other insecurities as well.

2. Learn to Love Yourself and Accept All of You

The next key I can give you concerning killing the assassin of insecurity is to learn to love yourself and to accept all of you. Even the people you think have the perfect life, the perfect body, and the perfect everything deal with insecurity because no one has everything and some of the greatest insecurities can't be seen with the naked eye. One of the greatest practices you can create, then, is to stop focusing on the pieces you don't have and to start focusing on the masterpiece that you are, built one of a kind for a unique purpose that no one else in eternity will ever be able to complete. Never before or never again will someone have your fingerprint or your combination of traits, talents, and abilities. You have so much to celebrate but your focus on what you lack is causing you to miss what you have.

It's like taking something small like a nickel or a dime and holding it out in front of you as far as you can. If you do so, you'll notice that the coin takes up very little of your vision and you may barely notice it at all. But if you close one of your eyes and you take that same small coin and you move it closer and closer to your open eye, you'll notice that it begins to block your vision more and more until the small coin gets just on the other side of your eyelid and you can see nothing at all. When you focus on small things enough, they cause you to miss everything else that is happening around you.

I wish I could sing like the greats, and if I could, I would pursue that with everything that I have, but the reality is that I can't sing because singing isn't my gift. But perhaps I spent my whole life holding a microphone and trying to overcompensate for a gift I wasn't given and tried to make myself become a singer. If I did so, I would never discover that with that same microphone I had the ability to operate in my true gift of speaking and inspiring others. If you suck at something, it's not the end of the world, but instead of always reminding yourself of that reality, find what gift you do have and that will make up for everything you don't. Perhaps your greatest discoveries about yourself are closer than you think. On a practical note, use the lines below to write down three things you love about yourself and spend time each morning or night verbalizing those three things and practicing self love.

THREE THINGS I LOVE ABOUT MYSELF

1. ______________________________

2. ______________________________

3. ______________________________

3. Surround Yourself with Supportive People

As discussed in the section on the assassin of association, who you surround yourself with has major consequences and will push you toward or pull you away from your purpose, and this running truth is important all the more as we work to kill the insecurities that are holding you back on your journey. Remember, our minds are like a garden and the thoughts, words, and beliefs instilled in us by others are seeds that will grow if watered. With that in mind, the fastest way to make your insecurities grow bigger is to surround yourself with people who water your insecurities with their words or actions, and the fastest way to make your insecurities die is to surround yourself with people who starve your insecurities of the water and the nutrients they need to grow by affirming you and supporting you in a healthy way.

Please understand that in speaking of people who water your insecurities, I am not talking of those whose mere confidence makes you feel insecure but rather those who reinforce the negative beliefs you already have. Until you find security in your own value, and maybe you have experienced this before, secure people may intimidate you, but instead of distancing yourself from them, find out where their confidence stems from and mimic that. For myself, I find my confidence in my relationship with God believing that he made me exactly how I was supposed to be, equipped me for everything he called me to do, and will provide all that I need when I need it. Because I believe those truths, I walk with a confidence that some may misinterpret as arrogance at times, but nonetheless I simply know who I am and where I'm going, so I don't slow up for anyone. Use the lines below to list three supportive people you have met in your life who you are committed to growing closer to and spending more time with. Deepening these healthy bonds will feed your confidence and starve your insecurities.

THREE PEOPLE I WILL GROW CLOSER TO

1. ________________________________

2. ________________________________

3. ________________________________

4. Practice Self Approval vs. Crowd Approval

Another major cause of insecurity in the lives of many is a person's dependency on others for approval. If they post their favorite picture on Instagram, they assume the picture was bad if they don't get the amount of likes or comments they tell themselves is good enough for acceptance when, in reality, dozens of people probably hadn't even seen the picture yet. If they tell their friends a funny story that happened in their life and they don't get the amount of laughs or the response they desired or expected, they start to feel insecure about themselves when, in reality, the group may not have understood correctly or may have just had a long day. Our desire to attain the approval of others for our worth places us in a rat race that will always leave us fatigued and unable to live life to the full.

The contrary to crowd approval, then, and the optimal position for each of us to live lives in which we aren't competing for the approval of others, is to learn how to affirm ourselves by knowing our worth. As I said before, "when you are whole before you hustle, the world can't distract you from the true mission and calling you were born to fulfill." As long as you're working for someone else's approval, people will manipulate you into their agendas for you to get it and can cut you off at any moment they desire, but when you wake up in the morning and say, "I know who I am and I know what I'm worth," you're prepared to run in your lane and you don't have to stop running to see what other people think because you can get that approval from yourself. By no means, however, I am suggesting that you approve of your actions that are wrong or immoral but only that you get to a place where you're confident whether "they" like you or not because you're not doing it for their approval. If you stay on your own vibe, you'll find your own tribe.

5. Kill the Comparison Game

The last piece of advice I will offer in this section of the chapter concerning killing the assassin of insecurity is to kill the comparison game. We live in an era where social media allows us to see what everyone else is doing, when they're doing it, no matter how far across the world they're doing it from. From live streams, to edited videos, to filtered pictures with big smiles, everyone can portray that they're living their best life and when you see this, you often feel as though you're not living yours. We see a picture from an angle they chose with an edit they made and it tells a thousand words, but more often than not it leaves out a million. Because of the human infatuation with living vicariously through the lives of our favorite Instagram accounts, however, we're left stuck in insecurity when we can't keep up with what they are portraying. If most of your days are spent watching someone else build their life, you're probably not building yours.

The question then becomes, how do we overcome this comparison game? If social media is the wave everyone is on, how do we stay in the loop without getting sucked into the loop in a way that waters our insecurity? How do we witness the seemingly glamorous lives of others while at the same time continuing to live our normal, seemingly mundane days? The secret is to FIND YOUR AWESOME.

Instead of drooling over their profiles and awesome lives while sitting on your couch at three in the morning eating a bowl of cereal, you get off the couch, you discover the gifts you have, you find the mission you were called to, and you run toward the vision God will upload into your spirit with everything you have. Perhaps you'll choose to document it or perhaps you won't. Nonetheless, the only way to stop comparing yourself to someone else's lane is to get off the sideline and run in yours. When you get a glimpse of your purpose, there becomes no time to look left and right because you're busy building your own thing. If you will use the tools described in *The Purpose Playbook* to find and follow your life's purpose, the deadly killer called comparison will die because you won't have time to feed it.

ASSASSIN 5: ACCOUNTABILITY

Think for a moment about one of the last times you had some dream or some major goal you sought to accomplish that after a period of time evaporated from your mind and was forgotten about completely. Perhaps it was New Year's Day and you purchased that gym membership telling yourself that you were going to lose thirty pounds but after a week or two something came up, your motivation was gone, and you quit. Perhaps you had a great idea for a book and you wrote the introduction and you started writing the first chapter but eventually got busy, swore you'd finish it later, and here you are, after years have passed, still having not picked it back up to start writing again.

In both of these cases, you had a major goal and a vision, perhaps you had a plan and believed that writing that book, starting that business, or enrolling in that program was a part of your purpose but even with all that…you quit. The motivation was there when you started. The vision was clear in your mind. You knew that you ought to do it and believed it was possible because you'd seen so many others succeed before you, but when it came down to it, all of those elements combined weren't enough to sustain you, and you quit. Why? While there could be a number of variables that I do not mean to disregard, one extremely common reason why a person who has everything lined up still gives up or fails is that they had no accountability.

Think about this for a moment. Let's say that your singular focus was to lose thirty pounds. You had the gym membership, the meal plans, the supplements, and you even bought the new outfit. With every tangible thing you need to be successful readily available to you, however, you have to understand that eventually the motivational high is going to fade, that early alarm you set is going to go off, and you're not going to want to get out of bed. But let's suppose that you do. Let's suppose that you make your way to your bathroom mirror to make the official decision to get back in bed or to go to the gym. Which of the following two mental conversations is more likely to ensure you get to that morning workout?

> Conversation One - "I never actually told anyone about my new goal but me, so if I skip today, I'm not letting anyone down. Besides, I can just work harder tomorrow, and I'm giving a presentation in class this afternoon so it's probably important that I don't show up tired. It's settled, then. I'm going back to bed."

> Conversation Two - "I'm tired right now and don't want to go to this workout, but I told Jason that I was going to meet him there, and I can't let him down. I really don't want to have to tell him that I bailed just because I was tired, so as exhausted as I am, I'm going to suck it up, get in the car, and go work out."

Do you see how much different the two scenarios were because of the presence of accountability? In conversation one, not having anyone to report to made it easy to make excuses and to attempt to justify those excuses, as humans do, by making claims that we'll overcompensate later or that doing what we know we should do may negatively impact something else like an afternoon presentation. In conversation two, however, the presence of accountability made the decision easy to make, though the person was tired, because the feeling of having to let down their accountability partner and say that they skipped the workout because they were tired was a much less desirable option than toughening up and working out even though the person would rather sleep.

It's easy to look yourself in the mirror and say I'll do it later, but when you add accountability to the equation, you make not attaining your goal difficult.

Did you catch that? By compounding your goal or vision with requiring yourself to give an account of your progress to reliable individuals, you make it difficult to fail. Imagine, then, if you surrounded your goal with not one but two or three accountability partners, meaning that if you wanted to quit or slack, you would have to call or comfort each of them and say, "I didn't do what I was supposed to do," because of the system of accountability you set up.

What is your vision in life at this point? If you don't know yet, that's okay, for later chapters are dedicated toward the crafting of your vision and discovery of your purpose, but for now, make a list below of five people you know who you believe are qualified accountability partners because of their integrity and reliability.

While most will not do this, those who desire real results should write beside each name the exact date (and location if applicable) they will ask this person to hold them accountable to the fulfillment of their vision and, together, decide how often (weekly, monthly, etc.) you will give them a report of your progress. If a person cannot commit, replace their name with another prospect until you have five solid commitments. This extra step is sure to boost your efforts because accountability keeps us efficient.

MY TOP FIVE ACCOUNTABILITY PARTNER PROSPECTS

1. ______________________________
2. ______________________________
3. ______________________________
4. ______________________________
5. ______________________________

ASSASSIN 6: THE FEAR OF FAILURE

There's an old war story of a man who was captured by the enemy army and was taken before the captain of the enemy. Upon his arrival, the captain said to him, "Tomorrow I'm going to give you two choices: you can either face the firing squad, or you can walk through this black door." Like most would do in that situation, the man said to the captain, "What's behind the black door?" But the captain said to him, "No one knows. Perhaps unspeakable horrors. Now tell me which you will choose: the firing squad or the black door." The prisoner thought for a moment, and finally told the captain that he would face the firing squad, and the next day the firing squad carried out their duties, executed the man, and reported back to the captain. At this, the assistants of the captain stopped him and said, "Sir, tell us what is behind this black door. Tell us what is behind this black door that no one ever seems to choose." After a long pause, the captain looked them in the eyes and said these words: "Freedom…but I've known few men brave enough to take it."

Each and every day of our lives, most of us, most people around us, most people in our family, most people in this world choose the firing squad. It's not that we want to or that we feel good about the idea of it but rather that we choose what we know is guaranteed instead of choosing the black doors in life when, in reality, behind the black doors are our dreams, our desires, and our purpose. Because of the assassin of the fear of failure, however, we settle for the firing squad day by day.

Before we continue and discuss the fear of failure in more detail and outline a plan of attack to eliminate it, use the lines below to write out a black door in your life–something you desire to do in which the fear of failure or of the unknown is the only thing holding you back.

MY BLACK DOOR IS

Remember the words of Les Brown that "people fail in life not because they aim too high and miss but because they aim too low and hit." No matter what your present situation looks like right now, no matter your age, no matter your background, your life has no shortage of opportunities that could propel you to another level–dates with destiny that could change your life forever which perhaps you have passed up time and time again because they looked like black doors in which the other side was unknown. These appear in the form of big doors but also in small ones as well. I challenge you, then, to make a habit of neglecting the firing squad and choosing the black door even if it's something as simple as talking to that person you've always wanted to talk to, posting that video of you singing that you've always wanted to post, or applying for that job you've always wanted to apply for. One date with destiny could change your life and at the very least will give you more confidence to walk through bigger black doors in the future.

As a friendly reminder, please understand that this chapter and my message is not to make you believe that someone is better or worse because of the size of their goal or the size of the black door they are planning to walk through. The narrative is not that the opportunities and dates with destiny I am describing are to be measured solely in terms of money, status, fame, or anything of the sort. The mission of this chapter is simply to get you to stop aiming below where you were created to aim and to get you to stop choosing your life's aim because of fear and the other assassins that haunt you but rather to choose your life's aim because of faith and because of the power of the God who called you to these big doors in the first place. You get one shot and life on this Earth and because of this, it's time, in the words of Mark Batterson, to "stop living as if the purpose of life is to arrive safely at death." You're not here by accident, so stop living like it. You're here because you were sent and because you have an assignment to complete.

To make this topic of the fear of failure more practical, I would like to discuss three major reasons why people fear failure in order to allow you to identify which aspects mentioned apply to you, thus giving you the opportunity to create the self-awareness needed to address the problem and the practical tools necessary to do so.

1. The Pain of Failing in the Past

Perhaps there has been some time in your life when you have failed, or fallen short, in some area. Often times, these experiences cause us to fear trying again because we feel that the pain of failing a second time would be worse than the pain of the first. For example, it could be a teenage girl who gets her heart broken in a relationship and decides to close herself off to people completely because the risk of getting hurt again seems stronger than the possibility of finding someone who will treat her how she deserves. Even more serious, it could be the adult who, after thirty years of marriage, gets a divorce and the sting of that experience hurts so bad that the idea of dating again, and even more so the idea of trusting someone again, seems inconceivable so they give up on relationships all together to avoid the pain.

Unless you've lived under a rock, you have probably heard of a man named Michael Jordan who is never left out of the conversation concerning who the greatest basketball player of all time is. Ironically enough, at one point in high school, Michael Jordan didn't make the team. Instead of letting failure or seeming defeat deter him, however, he bounced back and got better. "When I got cut from the varsity team as a sophomore in high school, I learned something. I knew I never wanted to feel that bad again. I never wanted to have that taste in my mouth, that hole in my stomach. So I set a goal of becoming a starter on the varsity."

Have you ever felt those feelings after being rejected? That taste in your mouth? That hole in your stomach? Notice how at a time when many would quit altogether because of the pain or embarrassment of public rejection, Michael Jordan let failure push him toward success, not away from it. Imagine if he gave up when he was told he wasn't good enough. History would have been robbed of a legend. In the same way, I challenge you not to give up on your dream the first time you hear, "No." Failure is not final if you don't let it be, but failure does have the ability to give you a hunger for success and for greatness that you didn't have before. Next time you fail and the voices in your head tell you to quit, reevaluate your goal, and if it's what you really wanted, then get up, get better, and go get it.

The problem, however, is that sometimes the voices telling us to quit are not internal voices in our head but rather are coming from the outside. Often times, the biggest challenge we face in fighting off that urge to quit at the first sign of defeat is that we have surrounded ourselves with so many voices and so many people that are always reminding us of the times we've failed, the times we've fallen short, and why this next time will be no different. If you've ever experienced this pushback, listen to me when I tell you to mute those voices and mute them fast.

Not every single person is going to understand the dream, the vision, and the purpose that you're cooking up in the kitchen. Not every single person is going to understand the ingredients that you're mixing up: the time, effort, dedication, faith, persistence, and drive you have, but if you listen to every single voice that is talking, gossiping, and reminding you of the times you failed in the past, you won't realize it but when you go back to start cooking in the kitchen again, an ingredient called fear will have fallen in and poisoned your recipe for success.

Why is this case? Because people who aren't living their dream can't stand to see you live yours. They're okay with you dreaming small, thinking small, and "staying on your square," but the moment you start to break out, they start to break down and try to shoot your dream out of the sky, and if you're not careful, you'll let them do it. If you're not careful, you'll stop when they say to stop and quit when they say to quit. These are not the voices of purpose and these are not the voices of God. Yes, you may have failed, but every successful person knows that you will fail your way to success. On the most practical level possible, the key to killing the assassin of the fear of failure that comes in the form of the pain of failing in the past is to cutoff the voices that remind you of the pain of your past and to replace them with voices, even if it's nothing but your own, that you remind you of the greatness that is within you and the vision God gave you in a whisper.

2. A Lack of Exposure to What is Possible

Another major reason people fear failure is quite simply that they have no exposure to all that is possible for their life. If you've never seen anything great happen for anyone else, it makes sense that you would be skeptical about risking the comfort of normalcy and blasting out into the unknown. But when you catch a glimpse of how limitless the possibilities are for your life and you begin to expand your vision even more, you begin to realize that the mind God gave you is enough to flip the world and your life upside down.

On the flip side, however, failure to expose yourself to what is possible sooner than later will cause you to, as mentioned earlier in this chapter, sprinkle your "*okay*" dust on everything God is trying to do in your life and on the extraordinary purpose he is calling you to. When an opportunity comes your way, you say, "I'm okay." When the dream you dropped long ago crosses your path again, you say, "I'm okay." Every single time the chance comes for you to take your life to another dimension not just for you but for your children's children, you say, "I'm okay." Why? Because you have grown accustomed to settling for everything in your life, but what if God has created, crafted, and called you for something more, for something bigger? What if the limits on those around you were not your limits at all? What if your biggest dreams would happen if you stopped settling left and right? What if you were not born to be "okay?" What if you have been lying to yourself and have been being lazy and calling it humble? I was not born to be *okay*. I was born to be obedient to the purpose and the call on my life and that means that if I'm called to aim high and I decide to aim low, that, by definition, is not called humility. It is called disobedience.

For someone reading this right now, you're settling for everything because there was something in your life that you wanted and that you went all in on, and it failed, so you lost hope because you don't want to experience that feeling again. Whoever you are, try again. I know you went to the conferences, you watched the videos, you read the books, and all of the gurus told you that, "It's your time," so you went for it, and it didn't work, and now you're confused and discouraged thinking, "I thought it was my time. Is it not my time? It must not be my time." Listen, it is your time, but it's God's timing. Time is macro while timing is micro. It's your time to build that vision, pursue that purpose, and follow that dream, but it's in being faithful in the season of "your time" that you will come to find that timing was around the corner, lurking, and waiting to hit you in a precise moment. Why? Because destiny catches a person in consistency.

Just because you failed last time doesn't mean you had the wrong idea. Perhaps the only thing missing was the wind behind your back that will come with the perfect timing, but you're going to miss it because your project didn't work the first time so you "quit." You don't want a good thing at a bad time. If you believe that the vision you are holding in your hand and the pursuit that perhaps failed before is, in fact, what God has given you, then keep working because the wind is coming and will take you to new heights if you're ready.

Don't miss destiny because you lacked consistency. No creator creates something with the intent that it would fail and neither did God create you without giving you everything you need, in the precise moments you need those things, to succeed. This doesn't mean that every "good" thing you attempt is going to work which is actually good because, by definition, "succeeding" at the wrong thing is actually failure. But whoever you are that is at the point where you must decide to give up or continue, I'm urging you to dare to fly again because it's your time, but it's God's timing.

3. A False Definition of What Success Is

The final element to be discussed concerning why people fear failure is that most people in this world have a false definition of success. There is nothing inherently wrong at all with making a fortune, acquiring mega fame, power, or anything of the sort, for often times those are the consequences of impact, but this does not change the fact that success is "the purpose of a thing fulfilled." This means that you could make millions of dollars and still fail in life because you missed your purpose, and it also means that you could be a megachurch pastor who gave your life to vocational ministry only to find that you missed your purpose because you went but were never called and therefore abandoned the post you were created for.

Become effective in your calling and money will come, but God forbid the world look at you like the biggest success of all time while you go home at night miserable out of your mind because you gave your life to something you were never created for. When you change your idea of success and understand, on a practical level, that you become a success when you do what you were created to do and that you are equipped with everything you need to be the best *you* of all time, your fear of failure begins to shrink because all you have to do to succeed is stay in your lane or get back in it when you fall out of it.

The six assassins described in this chapter desire to hunt you down and eliminate you on the path to your purpose. It was intentional that this information on developing the purpose mindset was placed at the beginning of this book to be read and studied before we enter into the purpose discovery process because much of the battle for your purpose is in your mind. Practice diligence while reading the upcoming chapters on finding and following your unique purpose, and you will be given valuable tools and information necessary to piece together the puzzle that is your purpose.

PART 2

DISCOVERING YOUR PURPOSE

LESSON 3

MASTER YOUR PAST

While the previous chapters have dealt with building a mindset that allows you to find and follow your purpose, this chapter and the pages that follow will have a much more practical focus on the question millions around the world are asking: "What is my purpose?" While I'm sure you understand that there is no magic formula which would allow you to click a few buttons and discover your life's purpose, and while everyone's journey will differ as each person's life takes them to a different place, I would like to first walk you through my journey with the intent of showing you how I found my purpose or, more accurately, how my purpose found me. In the stories I'll share, you will see how pain led to purpose and how dots connected in a way that could only be seen looking backward, never forward.

My twin sister and I were born on December 15, 1997 in Dallas, TX, but my earliest memory took place five years later on January 1, 2003. It was New Year's Day, and I remember my mother, my twin sister, and myself leaving a friend's New Year's gathering and coming home for the night, not knowing that our entire lives were about to change forever in a way that nothing or no one ever could have prepared us for. With smiles on our faces, we walked up the front door and walked inside, but when we did so, something was terribly wrong. At five years old, I looked up to the wall just past the doorway, and I saw before my eyes my father hanging from the wall just after he took his life by suicide.

None of us asked for a story like this, no kid deserves a start like this, and no person is prepared to deal with a reality like this. I remember like it was yesterday staring at the wall, not running, not crying, not yelling, and not moving at all. I just stood there and, with a five year old mind, tried to process what was happening until the tears rushed down my face when I realized that I would never see my father again. As best as you can, I need you to try to comprehend that as I write of this story fourteen years later, it can come off as "adversity I had to overcome" or "a challenge that made me stronger," both of which are true, but this was also a real experience that happened in real time by my five year old self who had no clue in the world that his purpose would one day come out of his pain.

As time passed, my mother, my sister, and myself did everything together and held each other close because, truthfully, family was all we had. Soon after, we enrolled in a school in Grapevine, TX called Faith Christian School that would be a major backbone for our family. While I gave my life to Christ as a second grade student at this school, however, I was still broken from the events which took place years before, I still felt misunderstood, and I still cried myself to sleep often. I still stepped into a shell that I put up, and I still walked around the hallways with voices in my head telling me that everyone around me was looking at me and thinking, "That's the kid whose dad died." It wouldn't be until years later that these chains would start to break off.

As I got older, I placed my identity in sports, believed that football was my life's purpose, and was actively working to make that dream become a reality. The problem I faced, however, was that injuries always inhibited my progress. From smaller injuries that I would cover with a cast and keep playing to bigger injuries like my two surgeries in January 2014 and December 2014, I always had some sort of health issue, but it was because of these two surgeries that one of my first encounters with purpose would come in the form of an unsuspecting opportunity. There was a large youth event in the area which took place every year and which I had attended in years past. At the event each year, students would get on stage and share their stories, and I remember sitting in those crowds being wooed by the courage of these kids and thinking, "That's great for them, but I could never do that."

Sure enough, over a lunch with a friend who actually ended up being the man behind the events, he asked me if I would speak and share my story at the event that year. The idea terrified me, but not wanting to say "no" to his face, I told him that I would pray about it, and I had full intention to text him a week or so later and decline the request. As time passed, however, and as I thought about and prayed about the opportunity, I felt God speak in a whisper and say, "If you take this opportunity, I'll change your life forever." At that, I told him I would speak at the event and months later I got on the stage and shared my story, something that terrified me because I thought everyone would judge me, but it ended up touching so many lives and liberating me from the danger of a painful story never shared, just replaying over and over in the mind of the one who experienced it. Sharing my story for the first time showed me that I had a voice and a message that had the power to change lives, and for the first time, I caught a glimpse of my purpose.

As mentioned before, months passed by before finding out that I needed another surgery that December, and it was while I recovered from this second surgery, when my eyes were taken off of sports which I thought was my purpose and was pursuing with my all, that purpose was about to catch me when I least expected it. While lying in bed recovering, two decisions were made that changed my life forever and propelled me onto the journey I'm walking on now. The first decision was that instead of wasting my recovery time and feeling sorry for myself like I did in January, I wanted to do something productive, something that I had always wanted to do, and had always started but had never finished–write a book. So, while still on pain medication and bed rest, I got my computer and started typing for hours until those hours became days and until, some two weeks later, I had drafted my first book, a vision that had been pulling on my spirit for years (Remember, purpose is often found in the pull.)

The second decision I made was only possible because I wanted to be a rapper in middle school, so

I owned recording equipment which, interestingly enough, was in the room with me. With no plan at all and while still lying in bed, I plugged in the microphone, pressed record, and started speaking whatever words were on my heart, and out came words of inspiration, words of motivation, and words of purpose. I posted the freestyle talk online, and as people began to give me feedback, I realized that not only was I gifted at motivational speaking, but I loved it more than anything I had ever done in my entire life. Just like that, with everything I loved being taken away by surgery, God placed in my lap everything necessary for my true purpose to change lives with my voice.

Please note, however, that even though I caught a glimpse of my purpose, nothing crazy happened overnight. No one knew me as a motivational speaker, no one was trying to bring me on television or book me to speak. I was just a kid who found something he loved so much that money, status, and fame didn't matter, and because of this, I was able to fall in love with the process. Howard Thurman said, "Ask not what the world needs. Ask what makes you come alive because what the world needs is more people who have come alive." I found something that made me come alive more than any other thing in the world, and I knew it had to be my life's pursuit.

So, there I was with a new book written that would be self published in March of the next year, thus becoming my first little footprint in this industry, and what I find very interesting is that it was just days after completing the book and taking that leap of faith by stepping out on what I believed was my purpose that confirmation came. Why? Because confirmation comes when you take the first step, not before. It was after the book was completed that, while cleaning out an area of our house, we came across a box that contained my father's belongings–a box that had been in the same place for years, a location I passed by every day.

When we opened this box, we found inside of it nothing less than motivational speeches and writings from my father that he had written when he was my age, which was shocking because I never knew my father enough to know that when he was young, he was pursuing a similar purpose. I didn't start my journey to continue a legacy, but I believe the purpose I was born for had been crying out for so long to be picked up where my father left off, and even if there was no verbal communication for that to happen, purpose was bound to expose itself, even in a little box that had never moved for so many years. It wasn't opened beforehand because it wasn't meant to be opened until the time was right.

Remember, you take the first step, and confirmation will come second.

For the next year, I spoke for free wherever I had the opportunity, I continued to make recordings and content to inspire others, and I also began preaching as well. The more steps I took in the direction of my purpose, the more doors began to open. The more I put myself out there, thus creating the opportunity to fail publicly, the more people caught the vision and invited me to speak or to be a part of what they were doing. It's like walking with a candle. It's not bright enough to show you the whole journey but only the next step. If you take that step, however, the next step will be exposed by the light.

Every day, I worked on my craft and studied materials to help me grow and develop. I saved up money from book sales and reinvested it into my vision by renting out a venue to host my own event. I didn't start for numbers, so a lack of them could never stop me. I was just faithful with what I believed was my purpose. I was just consistent with what was in my hand, and sure enough, destiny would soon catch me in consistency. My videos were circulating online and eventually got in the hands of someone who knew someone else who had the ability to do something with the potential I had. The next thing I knew, I received a phone call to be on James

Robison's Life Today television show where I talked about America turning from darkness to light. Months later, the show aired, and before I even had the chance to wake up completely, I saw that my phone was blowing up with hundreds of messages and dozens of speaking invitations from around the world. Here I was, a freshman in college, who had never spoken anywhere but in his local Dallas-Fort Worth area, getting asked to speak around the world.

Knowing my life would never be the same, I began traveling the country speaking, and meanwhile I posted a last minute video on Facebook which was a two minute clip from the show, and before my eyes, it blew up around the world and today has been viewed more than 7.5 million times and has reached tens of millions of people. Do I say all of this to boast? Not at all. I say all of this to say that I caught only a small glimpse of my destiny while recovering from a surgery when my goals were to play football, I grabbed hold of that glimpse and ran for it with everything I had, and while being faithful in the process, I was caught by my purpose. Though your specifics will be different on your journey, the same will be true for you. The big will always be found in the little, and you'll see things you could have never dreamed of if you're faithful in the small moments of walking in your purpose when no one knows who you are or no one seems to care. Destiny will catch you in consistency.

Today, I know without a doubt that my purpose on this Earth is to help others find theirs, and that's why I'm writing this book. I lost my father to suicide because, even if just for a moment, he forgot that he had a purpose to be here on this Earth, and too many others are taking their lives every day for similar reasons. Even concerning those who are in less dark of a place, millions of people in this world have no idea what their purpose is, so they move with no aim or direction at all. I've done what I've done at such a young age because I found my life's purpose and vision and for years have been working with that singular focus while most people go their entire life with no focus at all, hoping to end up "somewhere good" by going with the flow. It doesn't work like that. You'll manifest your purpose when you discover it and move toward it day by day, inch by inch. It will be hard, and it will take everything you have, but I promise you there's not another thing in the world I would rather do right now than write this book with the knowledge that it's going to change lives around the world. Why? Because I was born for this, and when you find what you were born for using what's talked about in this book, you'll understand firsthand what I'm talking about.

Now that I have shared with you my story and have showed you how from humble beginnings I have been able to see dreams happen that once upon a time were just ideas in notebooks, I want to explain this concept of "mastering your past" that will be vital for your ability to find and follow God's purpose for your life. The concept of mastering your past essentially means that, contrary to the typical mantra of "forget the past," it is a very dangerous thing to forget the past without first mastering it by moving forward while glancing back enough to own it and to learn from it without dwelling in it. If you forget the past and move on, I believe you have wasted the past, but if you master the past, you neither waste the past or the pain you experienced, and the past loses its ability to master you.

For example, for some ten years, I never shared my story publicly because the lie in my mind was, "If you share it, they'll judge you." This lie trapped me in my pain and caused me to internalize all that I had experienced, but the very moment I shared it, I was freed from ten years of pain and found my weapon to change the world–all in one single moment. What did that moment look like? It looked like saying "yes" to an opportunity I was set on saying "no" to. It looked like choosing the black door instead of choosing the firing squad and discovering that my purpose was right behind the black door the entire time.

Remember, much of purpose discovery comes down to understanding that much of what you might have considered “coincidences” were actually God working behind the curtain to push you and shape you and guide you to your purpose. I’m not trying to tell you that something terrible you experienced is something to celebrate, for I wouldn’t wish what I had to go through on my worst enemy, but this is where it comes back to mastering the past. Don’t let what happened beat you up and get away with it. You may not understand why it happened, but from it, your pain will birth your purpose.

I want you to use the lines provided to list off five defining moments in your life. Perhaps they were tragic or perhaps they were positive. Think on those moments that altered your life in big or small ways. Think on those moments in your past that perhaps you have tried to slide under the rug instead of mastering.

This is the most important exercise thus far, so I need you to be honest with yourself, and if you need more space, find paper or a notebook. Don’t think for three seconds and say, “I don’t know what defining moments have occurred in my life.” This exercise requires your diligence and your willingness to think. What major events make up your story?

FIVE DEFINING MOMENTS FROM MY PAST

1. ______________________________
2. ______________________________
3. ______________________________
4. ______________________________
5. ______________________________

Holding in your mind the defining moments you listed, whether in this book or somewhere else, I want you to reflect on each one of them and look at them through the lens of the following three steps to mastering your past: knowing your story, owning your story, and sharing your story.

1. Know Your Story

One of the most important steps to understanding your purpose and the route you ought to take in the future is to look back enough to know the story of your past–not to dwell on it, but to know it. Unfortunately, most of us never take time to do this either because of the fear of facing what happened or even just because we get so busy with the happenings of today that we make no time to think about yesterday. The problem, however, is that God often reveals our purpose to us like a game of Connect the

Dots, showing us how different events that happened in our past connect and how together they form a cohesive picture. It's from the best of times but much more from the worst of times that we are shaped and molded into the person we need to be in order to be prepared for the purposes of our lives. If you feel you've walked through hell in your life, know that nothing you've been through will be wasted, and God will redeem the pain and push you toward your purpose.

Remember, the past of each of us is rich with lessons and clues that will guide us to our purpose, but if you never step past the bitterness or the sting of what happened, you'll "move on with your life" having missed the clues and having wasted the past that would have changed your future. So, holding in your mind the defining moments you previously listed, you need to think hard and spend time in prayer about how those dots connect. I'm not asking you to figure out why the bad things happened but only how the dots connect. To help you understand this, let me refer again to the story of my life to show you how I went about this exercise in my own process of mastering my past.

As I told you before, my passion and pursuit in high school was to play football at a high level, and because of my love for the sport and my lack of self-awareness because I hadn't tried other pursuits, I believed that my purpose on this Earth was found in sports. The problem I faced, however, was that countless injuries were always stepping in the way of my goals. My first major surgery was the result of a tear in my retinaculum, located near my ankle, but what was interesting about this particular injury was that, although it happened on the football field, it actually didn't happen in the midst of any collision or even movement. I was standing in position as a defense back, waiting for the play to start, when all of us a sudden I fell to the ground as if God reached out and touched my ankle. Not knowing what happened, I got up and tried to keep going for the next play, and the same thing happened. When the trainer looked at my ankle, he shook his hand, and when I asked him if my season was over, he said, "yes." Just like that, my love was taken away, and I was devastated because I couldn't see how the dots would later connect.

Fast forward, I worked hard to get healthy again, and I came back the next season better than ever and also more focused than ever because it was my junior year which meant college recruiting would be more serious than ever. After a successful season, I was talking to college coaches and was still focused on my dream to play at the next level. It was at this time, then, that I returned to the doctor who performed my ankle surgery at the beginning of the year just to get a post-season look at the ankle to make sure that everything looked and felt fine, and it did. Before I left, however, I casually mentioned that I had been dealing with some knee pain for the last four years but that it was bearable, and I had been playing through it. With no concern in his eyes, he suggested we get an MRI to make sure it wasn't anything too bad, and after doing so, he told me that my patellar tendon in my knee was 85% torn, and I would need surgery right away or could have walking problems if something else happened. Once again, my dream was shattered before my very eyes in a way that didn't even make sense, but again, the dots never connect looking forward but only looking back.

As I mentioned before, it was after this second surgery when my eyes were taken away from football that I lay in bed and simultaneously discovered my gift to speak and write, which would later be confirmed in an even more serendipitous way when we discovered the motivational speeches and writings of my father who passed when I was five but whose legacy and message I was born to continue. Why do I say all of this? Because if I had allowed the pain of having my dream shattered multiple times to make me grow bitter, I would have gone into that second surgery feeling sorry for myself again, just waiting for it to be over so that I could pursue sports again–a pursuit that perhaps I was infatuated with and even talented at but not to the level that I'm gifted at walking in my true purpose.

It was in being open to something new and noticing that too many "coincidences" were happening for me to believe that was all they were that I found my purpose. It was in an unexpected situation which involved laying in a bed, still on pain medication, and recovering from surgery that the call on my life was awakened. I didn't let the defining moments of my life vanish in the past. I took time to know my story which then made it possible to connect the dots of my story that led to my purpose. Your dots will connect in a different way than mine did, but if you will know *your* story and connect *your* dots, you'll find that they were never coincidences. They were strategically placed dots in time that create a map for your future sent by God.

Using the lines provided to brainstorm, journal, or do whatever works best for you, think specifically about the "coincidences" in your life as they relate to the defining moments you recorded earlier. Start connecting dots concerning doors that closed which perhaps weren't supposed to stay open and doors that opened which perhaps you haven't walked through because it didn't line up with your preconceived notion about the direction you thought your life would go. Remember, by looking back at the dots of your past, you will inevitably catch clues and pieces of the map for your future–the map of your purpose.

CONNECTING THE COINCIDENCES

____

____

____

____

____

2. Own Your Story

The next important step in the mastery of your past is to not only know your story but to own it, thus taking back the power from it. One of the defining moments of this step in my life was a decision I made in my mind to not waste my second surgery by feeling sorry for myself until I was healthy again. I realized that having the surgery was out of my control, but what I did about it wasn't. And this is the truth I need you to understand about whatever happened in your life: you may not have the opportunity to choose where life takes you, but you do, by all means, have the choice to decide if you will stay there. For years, I've told people these words that I learned from my own story that "you must refuse to let the misfortune of your past determine the fortune of your future."

Life may have happened to you, but now it's your turn to happen to life. Someone may have left you, but there's too much greatness in you that will be wasted if you get stuck crying over what you lost instead of getting up and going to get something new. Own your story and own your past, but don't sit in it, don't settle in it, don't cry in, and don't die in it. Les Brown said, "If life knocks you to the ground try to land on your back because if you can look up, you can get up." Your future can be greater than your past if you own your past and take back your power.

Think for a moment about the life altering events of your life that perhaps you've made a subconscious decision to avoid looking back to. While I'm not asking you to pitch a mental tent in that place, I am asking you to see what you can extract from it that will help shape you and direct you on your own journey of finding and following your purpose, even if the lesson learned is nothing more than what you don't want to do or become.

If your father left you when you were young or was emotionally unavailable, owning your past may look like making a decision that you will be a parent who is present, emotionally available, and raises your children with the type of love you were robbed of. If you worked hard to develop an idea and out of your excitement you shared it with someone who ended up stealing it from you, perhaps owning your past looks like acknowledging what happened, daring to dream again, and guarding your future ideas and dreams like treasure, not tossing it before swine. If you experienced a sever amount of bullying at some point in your life, perhaps owning your past looks like being intentional about standing up for others in a way you wished someone would have stood up for you, or perhaps your history of being bullied has developed in you so strong of a passionate discontent concerning the problem of bullying that you feel drawn to start an organization, write a book, or begin sharing your own story as we will discuss in step three.

My point is that when we own our past and examine it with diligence, we may discover very practical ways that our past can show us what we should do with our lives today, for your purpose is not one event or action that you will one day complete before having fulfilled your destiny. Rather, purpose is a journey on your very own Purpose Road in which the call on your life will take you to a number of spaces and places to fulfill a number of unique assignments and missions you were created to act upon.

3. Share Your Story

As I mentioned before, years after I lost my father to suicide, I was still walking through the hallways of my school feeling as though everyone who walked by was thinking in their mind, "There's the kid whose dad died." I knew my story and the tragic events that had unfolded, but I was yet to take the power from it because my story owned me instead of me owning it, and as a result, it controlled my thinking and my life. Remember, a bomb explodes because of what is on the inside of it, not the outside, and the same is true with holding the life altering events of your past in your mind. If you keep it to yourself, staying up each night replaying events in your head or thinking about every way you wish you had handled the situation differently, you rob yourself of all peace and will eventually explode and have a breakdown. The solution, then, and the most important step in mastering your past, taking back the power from what happened to you, and moving from a victim mentality to a victor reality, is to share your story.

More than ten years after my father's death, I had still never shared my story publicly but instead internalized all of my thoughts, feelings, and emotions. It was when our family friend, Ryan Young, asked me to share my story at the annual youth event I mentioned earlier that I had to make a decision that had the potential to change my life forever. Would I get on the stage and share my story even though the narrative in my mind was that doing so would cause people to judge me, or would I stay concealed in the walls I had worked so hard to build for ten years, ensuring that my story was safe with me? I'm thankful today that I made the decision to say, "yes," because while I didn't know it back then, my purpose and my future self were depending on me to break down my walls and share. I was nervous, I was scared, and I was anxious, but I knew I had to do it, and when I did so, my life changed as I learned that by sharing my story, it transformed into an asset that would change lives around world instead of a liability that plagued my mind and held me back from much of what was for me in the world.

It's not about being glad the events occurred, but about knowing that they did, owning that they did, and discovering how you can use what happened to change the lives of others by using your story of strength to help those who are in the same situation you came from and need the strength to endure. Today, I've shared my story on stages, in books, on television, and so much more, and my story has impacted lives across the globe, but none of that would have happened, and those individuals whose names I will never know would have been robbed of the hope I gave them, if I never said "yes" to the question I was asked during my sophomore year of high school at a low point in my life, "Will you share your story?" I wasn't asked the question when I was feeling like a victor, but I promise you that if you'll make victor decisions when your circumstances scream "victim," you'll change your life, you'll master your past, and inevitably, you will liberate others around the world to do the same.

Using what you know about your own story and life events, what practical opportunities do you have to share your story or to use your experiences to help those around you? Maybe you've experienced events that were tragic and want to use what you've learned from it to help others by writing a book, starting a blog, or even just opening up to a small group of two to three individuals, whether people you know and trust or people in a similar situation as the one you came out of.

On the contrary, maybe your experiences in life thus far have been void of crazy events and, as a result, you feel you don't have much to offer. If that's the case, I want you to consciously override that mentality and think about how even smooth times have shaped you and developed you and how you can take note of what practices have proven to be effective in your life so that you can continue to develop them, preparing you for your future on whatever route your purpose takes you on. Remember, never compare your story to the next person's because it's *your* history, not theirs, that will prepare you for *your* purpose. Using the lines below, brainstorm practical ways you can share your story in order to master your past.

PRACTICAL WAYS I CAN SHARE MY STORY

LESSON 4

SEARCH YOUR SOURCE BEFORE YOURSELF

Now that we've discussed how mastering your past and connecting the dots of the events that have happened in your life leaves clues concerning your purpose, it's time that we talk, on the most practical level of all, how you answer the question, "What is my purpose?" While many teachers and gurus will tell you that the best way to answer this question is to start by searching inside yourself, the reality is that this is only half of the truth because while a person may look inwardly at their unique makeup and design to predict their purpose, only a person's true creator can confirm it. In this chapter, we will search deep within you to discover your unique gifts and abilities, but we can only do that effectively if we first understand the gravity of searching God first.

Mind you, the process I'm going to take you through works, but as mentioned in the title of this chapter, it is a search and this search requires diligence on your part. Too many people throw out statements like, "I want to know my purpose" or "If I knew my purpose, my life would be so much better," but if you look at their life, every free minute of their day is not spent searching for the purpose they say they desire to find but rather is spent relaxing, watching Netflix, or scrolling through Instagram.

If you want to find your purpose, it's more than possible, but quit saying you want to find it if your actions say otherwise. As you read the pages that follow, then, I challenge you to think hard about the questions asked and to be diligent about the process outlined because doing so will inevitably change your life and lead you away from this "I don't know what to do with my life, but I know I'm not supposed to be doing what I'm doing now" reality you've been living in.

When Apple created the phone that perhaps you use every day, they built into that phone capabilities and features they thought to be necessary for that particular model, and they left out features that would not be needed. Why? Because anytime a creator creates something, it equips its creation with every single thing that it needs to fulfill its purpose, and it leaves out everything that creation does not need because adding extra resources for no reason would be foolish and would be a waste. In the same way, it is God who created you for a particular purpose, and for that purpose he equipped you with everything you need and made you exactly how you needed to be in order to have the opportunity to be successful in the fulfillment of the assignment for which you were sent to this Earth.

You weren't supposed to be taller. You weren't supposed to be a different race. You weren't supposed to have an upbringing that was easier or more difficult. Everything about you and about your life, God has been using to shape you into exactly who you need to be for your purpose. If you want to find your purpose, then, you have to discover how you were shaped. This is why, in the previous chapter, we examined your past and discussed how to connect the dots to master it, and in this chapter, we will examine your shape in order to discover your purpose.

The problem, however, is that as I mentioned before, too many people are being taught a false narrative that says that searching yourself first will lead you to your purpose, but unfortunately, this will still cause a person to miss the mark every time. To further explain this, suppose you had never seen an iPhone before and I gifted one to you and said, “Here’s a new phone. I hope you enjoy it.” When you eventually get it set up and find time to try it out, you very likely would be amazed at the seemingly limitless amount of features your new smartphone had. Perhaps you would download apps, stream music, try out the camera, edit some photos, use the calculator, and so much more. Even if you spent hours each day messing around with your phone and trying out the many things it can do, the reality is that there would still exist features you never discovered, hidden features that were not visible to the naked eye or on the home screen of the phone but would only be discovered if you contacted Apple and asked them to show you all that the phone could do, or if you studied with diligence the manual that Apple left for you in the box which most people throw out without ever reading. You discovered so many new features that you were beyond satisfied, but still you didn’t even scratch the surface of all that your new phone could do. Such a high price was paid for the device, and you only tapped into a fraction of its capabilities.

Sadly, more often than is the case with the iPhone in the above example, this is what happens when our search for our life’s purpose starts with ourselves. We may discover amazing gifts, talents, and abilities that amaze crowds and bring us fulfillment, leading us to believe that we have found what we were put on the Earth to do, but our ignorance is found in the fact that only our creator could show us everything that he built into us, but we didn't go to him, nor did we search the manual he left for us. Using this common strategy, many find worldly success because gifts are gifts and do what gifts do, but they miss their true purpose because there was more inside of them that they never discovered.

I'm writing this book to tell you, whoever you are, young or old, black or white, rich or poor, considered by society to be a success or a failure, there is more inside of you. Perhaps you've already achieved a degree of worldly success and are pursuing a dream of yours. I would dare to say that there's more inside of you. Perhaps you're a college student who desires to know their purpose and you think you know your gifts, but the two don't seem to click. I would dare to say that there's more inside of you. Perhaps you're a single parent who's working while raising two kids, and you feel stuck in a cycle you want to escape but simply can't. I would dare to say that there's more inside of you. We're going to search what's in you, and we're going to find it, but in order to reach your potential and to step up to levels you've never dreamed of, we have to start with your creator and see what he built into you.

If you don't have a relationship with God already, now is the time to form one and to begin studying his Word, the manual he left for you. The closer you get to him by building a relationship through time and communication like you would with any other person, the more his light begins to illuminate things you didn't know you had, and he begins to open doors that you could have never manipulated your way into. As you study his Word, be careful to do so with diligence and consistency and to pray throughout your day. Without neglecting everything else, study the Psalms and the Proverbs, and read of how he formed you, crafted you, and gave you a purpose before you took your first breath or said your first word.

When you start here and you search your source first, it's like aiming a bow toward the bullseye. You may have had the sharpest arrow and the sharpest gift, but if you can't aim it correctly, you'll never hit the bullseye for your life and will likely miss the target as a whole. Keeping this in your mind and heart, I would like to introduce you to my very own purpose discovery process that I will call *The Four Circles*. Know them, study them, and follow them, for when viewed from a place of a true connection to your creator, these four circles will lead you to your purpose.

THE FOUR CIRCLES

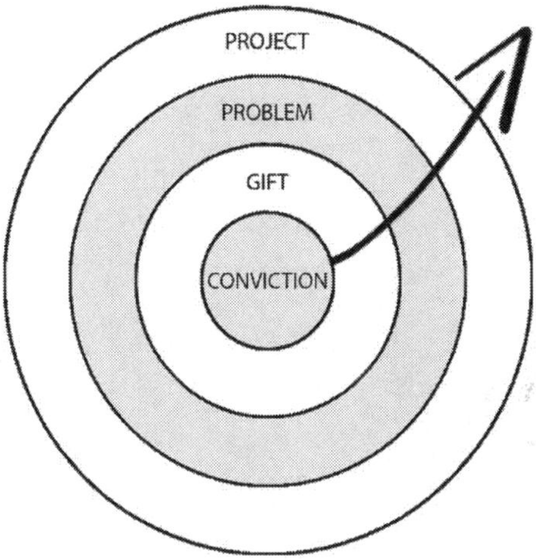

The four circles outlined in this diagram are as follows: your conviction, your gift, your problem, and your project. Before we begin, however, I would like for you to take note of the arrow which starts in the center and works its way out, indicating that this process only works if you do the same, beginning with the inner circle and working your way to the outer circle. For many, this will not come naturally because it's countercultural and our society trains us to choose our life's aim based on anything but our convictions, gifts, and problems to solve but rather often starts with questions like, "What project or pursuit will make me the most money or bring me the most security?" If you follow this new process, however, you will find that built into you by your creator are clues that will lead you not to a mere concept of purposeful living but to your personal, one of a kind life's purpose. This is a chapter you will need to refer back to or think about often, but when the four components described begin to click, so will your life, and so will your purpose.

CIRCLE ONE: FIND YOUR CONVICTION

Before we touch on anything else, we must begin with the inner circle and you must objectively analyze and purify your conviction. This refers to your conviction about yourself, your conviction about your God, your conviction about your potential, and so much more. Unfortunately, it matters little if you master every other circle in the diagram if your convictions are out of line because gifts, for example, mean nothing if the one who has them doesn't believe in them, and this is where millions of people get stuck when it comes to finding and following their purpose. Everyone can see their aptitude and impact in a particular arena of life, but their conviction about themself is so poor that they never walk to their purpose with boldness. Why? Because even if everyone in the world believes in you, if *you* don't believe in you, the natural outcome is that you will fall back to *your* conviction, not to theirs.

You can read the books, you can watch the inspirational videos, and you can make some motivational quote the background on your phone, but if your conviction of yourself does not change for the better, nothing happens. What do you believe about yourself? What do you believe about your potential? Do you believe that you can succeed despite growing up around failure? Do you believe that you were born for a purpose despite looking around the world and seeing so much chaos? Do you believe that you can find that purpose and change your life? Your beliefs, no one else's, will steer you to success or failure in life.

Furthermore, you must analyze and purify your conviction about your God. Have you allowed a bad experience with church or legalistic religious people to taint your view of the God who created you and possesses the ability to move on your behalf in order to position you to fulfill the call he's given you? Do you believe that God is for you and not against you, even though you've been through challenging circumstances that perhaps have developed you into a soldier ready to fight for your purpose? Do you believe in God? Not only that he's real but also that he's working in your life and on your behalf?

Remember, the beliefs and convictions of those around us are not what alters our life but rather our beliefs and convictions that we hold in our own mind. If you want to be successful based on our definition of "purpose fulfilled," it is imperative that you develop a success consciousness, or a purpose consciousness, in which you believe in yourself not because those around you do or don't believe in you but rather because you caught a glimpse of the purpose for your own life and understand that if you follow it, though it will be a challenging road, it's yours before you get it.

You must develop a thought pattern that takes thoughts captive as they appear, judging each thought by the question, "Does this align with my conviction or conflict with it?" Mind you, the convictions you hold must first be purified and corrected, but if your thoughts don't pass the test once you develop the winning mentality of a person on a mission, you must dispel them immediately before they take root.

Using the lines provided, write at least two sentences describing your convictions about yourself, about your God, and about your potential. Don't answer the question how you would if asked by a stranger walking down the road, telling them that you believe in yourself if, in reality, you don't. Write the deep thoughts of your mind that hide in the back of it. Write the faulty narratives in your head that speak up and attack each time you think about the possibility of you succeeding in life. If you can be honest about your convictions, we can be precise and effective in correcting them.

MY DEEPEST CONVICTIONS ABOUT MYSELF, GOD, AND MY POTENTIAL

____

____

____

____

____

Looking at what you wrote, I want you to draw a star next to each conviction that you know is not helping you succeed in your life. Perhaps you wrote that you believe you are too old, or even too young, to follow the path that is tugging on your soul. If this is the case, for example, you should understand that the only thing disqualifying you from that dream you have is your conviction. Sure, there are many pursuits and paths that have requirements such as the many years it takes to become a doctor, the processes and levels one goes through to become a professional athlete, or the age one must be to drive a car on the road, but the reality of life is that many of the limitations we rehearse in our mind are self imposed, and if we can identify them, we can eliminate them.

Keeping this in mind, the next step to developing a purpose consciousness is to focus your mind, daily, on convictions that will positively influence your journey to becoming everything you were meant to become. Using the lines provided on the following page, write five "I AM" statements which speak not to your present but to your future.

For example, if your prior conviction was that you are too old, or too young, to become an author, I want you to write on one of the lines below, "I am a bestselling author" or something of the sort that pushes past your prior beliefs and forces you to expand your vision of what you could become.

If your prior conviction was that because you didn't go to school, you could never run a successful business, I want you to write on one of the lines below, "I am a successful business owner of XYZ Company," and then begin absorbing the limitless amount of free resources that are available to you, whether physically or online, which could possibly help you more than a degree or the formal education system would have.

MY FIVE "I AM" STATEMENTS

I AM ______________________________

I AM ______________________________

I AM ______________________________

I AM ______________________________

I AM ______________________________

This simple practice works to destroy your self imposed false convictions by speaking past them and to your destiny. While most will skip this step, I recommend re-recording these "I AM" statements on a notecard and reading them out loud every morning and every night. In doing so, your statements will sink into your subconscious mind, causing you to believe and to act upon them, despite what others say or believe about you.

CIRCLE TWO: FIND YOUR DOMINANT GIFT

Upon developing convictions conducive for your success, the next progression in the process is to move to the second circle which is finding your dominant gift. Not a single person in the world was created without a gift, and each of us have actually been given multiple gifts which were placed inside of us before we were born in order that we might discover, direct, and deploy them into the world which would, in turn, propel us toward our purpose. One of the greatest tragedies, however, is that most people die without ever tapping into the gift that was given to them which had the ability to change their life and to change the world. For this reason, I ask you to navigate this section of the chapter with diligence as you work to discover your gifts and learn the power that is sure to come if you will use them.

In Proverbs, we see a powerful statement which says that "a man's gift," not his education but his gift, "makes rooms for him and brings him before the great." It says, "Do you see a man that is skilled at his work, he will not serve before obscure men." Our gifts are one of the most powerful tools that we have to change our lives and impact the world, but it's tragic that our society and education systems wire our thinking to believe that the key to success is formal education when you can have more degrees than a thermometer, a 4.9 GPA, and still be unable to find opportunities. Why? Because the key that opens doors for a person and makes room for them in the world, today more than ever, is not education but *gifts*.

If education was the key, everyone who was educated or had a PHD would be financially stable and would have a host of opportunities to choose from, but if you look around the world, that is obviously not the case. Education is great. Education is important, whether you get it formally or informally, but if you never tap into your gift, you'll be frustrated for the rest of your life because you were created to operate in it. If you do tap into your gift, however, prepare to see things you've never seen before and to walk through doors that your degree could have never opened for you, for it has always been a person's gift that makes room for them in the world.

While it seems simple in writing, the problem that people face on a practical level in pursuit of their own life's purpose is that they hear about the importance of finding and following their gift, but they either don't know what their gift is or they have an idea about a few different things they're "kind of good at" and they don't know which one to follow. The answer to this problem is that the idea that your gifts will lead you to your purpose is true but is only half of the truth. The missing piece of the puzzle that leads many to confusion is found in the fact that, of the many gifts a person has been given, even if they are yet to find them, it is their "dominant gift" that is to be discovered, directed, and deployed into the world, and it is this dominant gift that will propel them toward their purpose while many of their other gifts will play a supporting a role, smaller than that of their dominant gift.

While your gifts can be defined as those traits or abilities in which you excel most naturally, your dominant gift is best defined as "that which you do the absolute best with the least amount of effort." This dominant gift is what will open doors for you on the path of your purpose. It's what you will use most in your vocation in a way that others who lack the gift will try to replicate but will not be able to. It's what you will get paid for and is a reason you will need to make a practice of humility because you will also be loved for it in the eyes of others. Your dominant gift is your ticket to your purpose, but you must protect it because people will come for it, and not all who come for it will have right intentions.

Understanding this, I can imagine that many are still holding the conviction they've held for so long, "I still don't know what my gift is." The reason many find themselves stuck and frustrated in this conclusion is that our society has done a poor job of helping us identify the gifts that we have. If you had the voice of an angel or could run like the wind, I am sure you would have no problem at all identifying your gifts, but as long as we define gifts as running, jumping, singing, dancing, and having a high IQ, a kid fails a standardized test and thinks that he's stupid when, in reality, his gift simply could not be measured by a math test or a reading comprehension exam. But unfortunately, because the kid doesn't know that, he buries in the ground and never discovers all of the gifts that he had.

I wonder how many gifts are hidden in the inner city. I wonder how many gifts are hidden in the hood. Perhaps the cure for cancer is in the mind of a kid who will never discover it or bring it to the world because in fifth grade, he couldn't tell his teacher the degree count of an acute angle of an isosceles triangle, and she told him that he was stupid, and so he stepped into the words that she spoke. Why? Because our words have the power to speak life or death.

Many years ago, there was a kid who couldn't speak fluently until he was nine years old and his teachers thought he was slow, so they kicked him out of school. His name was Albert Einstein. Years before that, there was another kid whose teachers said that he was "too stupid to learn anything," but little did they know that "the stupid kid" would go on to invent the light bulb and to hold 1093 patents. His name was Thomas Edison. "If you judge a fish by its ability to climb a tree," said Einstein, "it will live the rest of its life believing that it is stupid."

If you can't identify what your gift is or if you

simply feel like you don't have one, then perhaps your gift is simply something that is not as common as the popularized running, jumping, singing, dancing, and being super smart. If math doesn't come naturally to you and someone wants to make you feel stupid for not being able to thrive at it, just walk away with a smile thinking, "Math simply isn't my gift, but when I find mine, I'm going to shine." By no means am I suggesting that you grow lazy and give poor effort in areas of your weakness but rather that perhaps our society's narrative that our weaknesses should get crazy amounts of extra help in order to get them to match our strengths is ridiculous, and the focus should be on having enough self awareness to know what you're not good at, to know what you are good at, and to spend your mental energy developing those strengths.

In his book, *Managing Oneself*, Peter Drucker says, "It takes far more energy to improve from incompetence to mediocrity than it takes to improve from first-rate performance to excellence." You can always build a team of people who specialize and are passionate about the areas you're not gifted in, but if you give your weaknesses all of your attention, you'll never find the time to become excellent at your strengths.

This leads us to a very important question and to

assistance for those who cannot answer it: what is your dominant gift? To find it, we must first know where to look and where not to look. Many don't know what their dominant gift is because all of their free time is spent scrolling through social media admiring the gifts of others or trying to replicate what is working for someone else because someone else's gift looks good on them, but this approach will always lead to frustration. If you gave me a thousand dollar tennis racket, the Nike uniform, the sweatband, and the fancy shoes while on the other side of the court was Serena Williams barefoot with an antique racquet from eBay, she would still beat me. And while it sounds funny, this is why so many never manifest their own greatness. They're always trying to replicate the gifts and greatness of others and, in their mind, can't separate the tools the gifted person uses from the gifts the gifted person has. It's true that world class people often use world class equipment, but you're not like Mike because you buy the Jordan shoes, you're like Mike because you are Michael Jordan, you have the gifts Michael Jordan has, and you developed them as skills over the course of time.

If you want to find your dominant gift and want to start living your life with it instead of living vicariously through the lives of others who have found their own gift, you first must understand that your gift won't be found on social media or on Google but rather inside of you. Why? Because God has planted seeds inside of you that possess your gifts. Seeds never look like much when they first start out, but the moment you discover them, you can start watering them, developing them, and watching them grow.

How do you discover these gifts? Just like a bird never watches a YouTube video on how to fly but rather was born with the fly built into it because it was purposed to fly, you look at what was inherently built into you, and that will lead you to your dominant gift and purpose. This may not look as simple as sitting on the couch eating cookies, closing your eyes, thinking, and coming to a spontaneous revelation of your gift. Rather, it is more likely to look like trying new things until you discover what you excel at most naturally. You can read the books, watch the videos, and take the surveys on "finding your gift" all day long, but until you try it, you'll never discover if you're truly gifted at it. This means humbling yourself and being willing to fail and to look bad trying things that may end up not being for you, but if in the end you discover your dominant gift, every failed attempt will be worth it hundreds of times over.

After discovering your dominant gift, the next vital step is to direct it. From the time of your birth until now and forever, the gifts that have been entrusted to you, those vital weapons that were given to you to impact the world and to shine light and glory on your creator will never and can never be taken back. What this means, then, is that if you decide to use your gift of song to spread messages of violence and evil, you have the power to do so, and the gift won't be taken away by the gift giver. If you have a gift to persuade others but decide to use it for manipulation, the gift will not be taken away. It also means, however, that when times come in your life and you find yourself having made a mistake or used your gift in the wrong way, even if it was doing the right thing for the wrong reason, all you have to do is realign your aim, turn your gift back toward the right path, repent of the wrongdoing, and begin deploying your gift into the world again which leads to another important requirement to operating in your purpose–embracing your gift.

Not everyone can sing well or run fast, but everyone has a gift to bring to the world, and far too many people never do so not because they never discovered their gift but because they didn't think it was anything glamorous and so they never embraced it. Martin Luther King Jr. said, "If it falls your lot to be a street sweeper, sweep streets like Michelangelo painted pictures, sweep streets like Beethoven composed music." Own your gift. If you're gifted to cook, aim to cook like Beyoncé sings. If you're gifted to organize events, aim to organize events like Usain Bolt runs. If you're gifted at doing hair and makeup or telling stories, work your gift like the best in the world worked theirs.

Too many people fall so in love with titles and positions that they seek promotions that increase their authority but remove them from the sphere of their gift's effectiveness, thus leading them to their failure. What a shame it would be to try to be the CEO when you were the best second or third in command that your company had ever seen, but the title of "CEO" made you fall in love and, when you got there, proved to be more than you were gifted to handle. Unfortunately, this is a harsh reality for many in every line of work because they fail to embrace what they have and would rather try to latch on to what worked for someone else.

Using all that you have learned on the previous pages, I would like to give you a chance to think about what your dominant gift may be that perhaps you've already discovered, perhaps you've discovered but never embraced, or perhaps you've never discovered at all. Preparing yourself with stillness, focus, and a readiness to analyze yourself objectively and honestly, think about what activity or action you are drawn to like a magnet that electrifies you when you operate in it, causing time to pass by seemingly faster than ever. Think about the strengths you have that come naturally to you but cause others to struggle and complain. On the line below, answer the following question to the best of your ability: what is your dominant gift? If you still can't answer the question, ask those closest to you what gifts they see in you, for those around us can often see parts of us that we can't see.

MY DOMINANT GIFT IS

Example: My ability to inspire others with my words.

CIRCLE THREE: FIND YOUR PROBLEM

After shaping your convictions and discovering your dominant gift, the next circle that is critical to finding and following your purpose is identifying your problem. Put simply, the type of problem I'm referring to is something in the world you were created to change, impact, or solve. As mentioned before, it was Myles Munroe who said, "Your existence is evidence that this generation needs something that is inside of you." You were sent here for a purpose at this particular moment in history, and there is something you were created to do in your time here that you would rob the world of if you died without discovering and following the reason why you lived. The challenge, then, is not that the world is short of problems but that the world is so full of problems that finding yours becomes difficult.

The solution, then, as we have done before, is to search the design that God created us with in order to discover what we were created to do and what problems we were created to attack. The solution is not to pursue something, even a noble pursuit, just because the world needs it, for this would keep you from doing what you were sent here to do in an effort to do what someone else was sent here to do. Better put and to better explain where this section of the chapter is going, let me remind you of the words of Howard Thurman who said, "Ask not what the world needs. Ask what makes you come alive because what the world needs is more people who have come alive." I'm not going to ask you what you're passionate about because the word "passion" has been too watered down in our society. Rather, I want to ask you this deeper question: what makes you come alive? What is it you love to do so much that when you do it, time goes by faster, you forget to check your phone, you forget to eat, you forget to sleep, and you would do it if no one ever paid you a dime? What subjects, topics, or problems trigger you when they arise in a way that someone else would shrug them off without feeling moved in the deepest parts of their soul as is the case with yourself? What brings out the truest version of you?

The reason I ask these questions is that I believe God has built into each of us passions and triggers that pull on our soul and pull us toward our purpose. The reason I'm writing this book right now and have dedicated my life to helping people discover their purpose is because I heard too many people, with pain in their eyes, say the exact same words, "I don't know my purpose," and the fact that millions are asking that question may not bother you, but it hurt me so bad that it moved me to action. It hurt me so bad to hear about people taking their life by suicide every single day, often times expressing the concern, "I don't feel there's a PURPOSE for me being here." It hurt me so bad to walk into the house at five years old and to see my father just after he took his own life by suicide because, even if just for a moment in time, he forgot that he had a purpose for being here and felt leaving was a better option. The problem of purpose is my problem that made me come alive and that I'm chipping away at every single day and that I know is a part of my own purpose. When you find your problem, you'll find your purpose.

Think for a moment about the question I asked you: what makes you come alive? Think about the triggers you have, the things you love, and the problems that keep you up at night of which you know in your soul you were created to be a part of the solution. Using the lines below, list one to three problems that make you come alive.

THE PROBLEMS THAT MAKE ME COME ALIVE

1. ______________________________
2. ______________________________
3. ______________________________

CIRCLE FOUR: FIND YOUR PROJECT

Having worked on your convictions, discovered your dominant gift, and identified your problem, we are now led to the outermost circle in *The Four Circles* diagram which is to find your project. One of the biggest problems that people face in discovering their purpose is that they have in their mind a picture of purpose that says, "One day, I'll discover my purpose out of nowhere, and it's going to come in the form of one word or one statement that says, 'you will do XYZ' or 'you will become XYZ.'" The issue, then, is that they've created an idea that purpose is one single moment in time, or one single event in time, that they will arrive at one day and find fulfillment. Because they've blown this one future event so far out of proportion, and because they feel so strongly that this one single event will be hit or miss, the whole idea of purpose overwhelms them to the point where they don't pursue it at all.

The reality, however, is that purpose is a long journey that I like to describe as Purpose Road, and along this journey of following your purpose, following your aim, and following your vision that is developed over time, you will come across opportunities and will encounter destiny, in big and small ways, throughout the course of your life. Your assignment on this Earth is not one event in the distant future while during the rest of your life you must just hope to one day get there. Purpose is a road and finding purpose is about finding *your* road, not a road created for anybody else.

To find your purpose, then, you must understand that throughout your life you will encounter life altering moments and, at times, bigger parts of the puzzle or future destinations will be revealed than at other times, but that does not change the fact that purpose is still a road and that purpose is still a process. The key, then, to purpose discovery is to discover the Purpose Road with your name on it, and you do that by positioning yourself on the correct road, diligently doing what is in your power, and allowing God to do his part.

On a practical level, you can do this by engaging yourself in what I would describe as purpose projects which are ideas, projects, endeavors, whether temporary or permanent, big or small, that allow you to use your dominant gift to progressively solve, change, or impact the problem that makes you come alive. This is why the other circles were so important, and why the order of the circles mattered so much. If you seek to solve a problem that doesn't make you come alive, you won't have the drive necessary to keep on going when the motivation fades. If you find a problem that makes you come alive of which you are not gifted enough to do anything about, you'll find yourself frustrated and fatigued because you're trying to open a door with a key that doesn't fit. If you find a problem that makes you come alive of which you are gifted enough to do something about, but your convictions about yourself or about your God are weak, you don't stand a chance at making any impact no matter how gifted you are because you'll lack the confidence to manifest your gift and the power of it regardless of how many people tell you that you can. If you master each of the circles, however, and you intentionally position yourself on your Purpose Road, you position yourself for God to propel you down that road at his pace, bringing you the fulfillment you've felt so empty without, the vision you've felt so lost because you lacked, and the hope for the future you're yet to know.

Remember, your project may be big or your project may be small. Your project may last a week or your project may last a lifetime. But it's not about your whole life's purpose being bottled up in one temporary project but about these projects positioning you on Purpose Road and causing you to operate in your purpose today. In an interview, T.D. Jakes spoke about a conversation he had with someone who told him that they had a dream to go into the music industry, they were about to graduate from their college in which they were studying music, but they wondered, "What if I do all of this, and it's not the thing for me?" In response, T.D. Jakes told him, "If it's not the thing, it will be the thing that leads you to the thing." That's what the purpose projects are about. If you are tapping into your gift, developing it in the process, and you are using your gift to solve problems God has placed deep within your soul which you are able to discern because of your connection to him, you are going to find yourself walking in your purpose. You are going to find yourself no longer lost because your purpose projects are leading you to a vision for your life today and are giving you glimpses of a vision for tomorrow, and you are going to change the world by changing your world in the spaces and places God has placed you today.

The key is that you must stay diligent in focusing on your purpose, not getting distracted by the purposes of others or the mere distractions and vanity of the world. If you stay faithful in working on your projects, not just any projects, but those that align with your purpose, God will see your faithfulness and will take you to new levels in your projects, in your vocation, and in your life as whole, not for you but for him. Find your project(s), work on it with diligence every day, and destiny will catch you in consistency.

The possibilities of projects to work on and ways to do so are only limited by your creativity. Some may start small projects that position them on Purpose Road like reading and learning about their problem daily, volunteering with a local organization, or creating a space for conversation to raise awareness about a particular issue. Others may start a blog, write a book that's been on their heart, or write a song that's been in their soul. Some may find that their projects look more like long term pursuits which could include enrolling for school to finish your degree or taking the job offer that pays less but is more in line with your dominant gift and chosen problem and will prepare you for the larger places your purpose will take you to in the future, while your former job wasn't doing that at all.

No matter your project, big or small, long term or short term, be diligent in it, take pride in your work, and know that everything in life is for but a season, but one project, one venture, one pursuit will always lead to the next. One project could be all you need to change your entire life forever. In volunteering for that club, you may cross paths with a person who notices your gift and has a connection to someone who can take it to another level. In writing that book and sharing your story, you may save the young person who is in the same situation you overcame and wanted to take their life but read your book and found hope. In taking that new job, you may learn a skill or meet a business partner who you end up starting a company or nonprofit with that takes your life to places you never imagined.

None of the above scenarios described are the reason why you engage in purpose projects but rather are the natural results that come from being on

Purpose Road. God has already placed the people, resources, and opportunities you need exactly where you need them on your journey, but if you're not on *your* road, you'll be like most people and miss out on all of them, not because they weren't present but because you weren't in position to receive them. If you're faithful in your small projects on Purpose Road, God is faithful and will entrust you with bigger ones you could have never dreamed of.

Using the lines below, write three purpose projects you would like to consider starting–projects that allow you to use your dominant gift to solve, change, or impact the problem that makes you come alive. Remember, they could be big or small, long term or short term, but if you're diligent, they'll lead you along the way of walking in your purpose and will change your life forever.

MY PURPOSE PROJECTS

1. ______________________________

2. ______________________________

3. ______________________________

Be serious and timely about deciding which of these projects you will work on, and upon making the decision, be diligent enough to follow through using everything you have learned and will learn in this book. You never know who or what is waiting on the other side of your decision to say, “yes” to your purpose project. The world is waiting on you. What are you waiting for?

PART 3

PURPOSE IN ACTION

LESSON 5

STOP TREATING YOUR GIFT LIKE IT'S A HOBBY

Imagine for a moment if Steve Jobs did nothing with his creativity and innovative thinking but instead decided to dabble in those gifts as side projects while following a more traditional path and getting a more traditional job. If this was the case, the world would have been robbed of all that Apple has become and of all the ways the company has changed the world. Imagine for a moment if the Wright brothers conceived in their mind the possibility of creating a machine capable of human flight, started building their vision, but gave up because of their limited resources or decided to move at a slower pace which would have caused someone else to build the machine before them. If that was the case, you and I would not be familiar with the names Orville and

Wilbur Wright because they likely would have become like millions of others throughout history who had a great idea but did nothing with it and were forgotten as a result. Imagine for a moment if Michael Jackson and his brothers discovered they had an amazing gift to sing but decided to make of it nothing but a hobby that would be witnessed only by the Jackson family. If that was the case, every person who has ever been moved by the family's music would have been without the experience the Jackson family was born to bring into the world.

What all of these people have in common that allowed them to change the world in the many ways they did is that each of them discovered their gift and developed it as a skill over time with a work ethic that most people in this world could never comprehend. It's easy to look at the final product and to admire the gifts that these individuals brought into the world, but each of them knew that gifting alone was not enough to make happen everything they manifested. The world is full of gifted people but many less see all that their gifts could be. Why? Because most people in this world who discover their gift treat it like a hobby. If you want to become the greatest version of yourself by fulfilling the call on your life and the reason you were sent here to this Earth, it's imperative that you take the gift you have and you develop it over time with practice and repetition, crafting it and shaping it so that it's ready for action when your encounter with destiny comes and the spotlight that could have changed your life destroys you because, like film on an old camera that needs to enter the darkroom, you brought a gift to the light that wasn't developed in the dark. If you want to manifest your purpose, stop treating your gift like it's a hobby.

Walt Disney said, "Whatever you do, do it well. Do it so well that when people see you do it, they will want to come back and see you do it again, and they will want to bring others and show them how well you do what you do." God did not give you the gift you have for you to keep it to yourself or only show those closest to you. Your gift was given to you to shine the light of God on others and will touch lives in ways you'll never know, but none of this is made possible if you treat your gift like a hobby and keep it to yourself. I know you're gifted, and I know that gift alone can take you far, but I also know that your gift developed will take you places you never imagined and will change the lives of people you'll never meet.

With that said, treating your gift as more than a hobby begins when you stop downplaying how much power is packed into what you have. Perhaps your gift doesn't look like the common gifts everyone celebrates, but I can assure you that the gift you have, even if it's one that most would never consider "cool" at first glance, is a powerful weapon waiting for someone to load it with ammunition. I don't care if your gift is your ability to change a tire faster and more effortlessly than anyone in your city. Just as scripture says, your gift will "make room for you." I don't care if your gift is your ability to memorize words with ease as evidenced by the fact that you can quote movies you watched years ago and can recite lyrics to songs you don't even listen to anymore. That gift will "make room for you."

The problem most have, however, is that they don't make room for it. They don't make room for their gift, so they never allow their gift to make room for them. Often times, this is because they don't give their gift enough credit as to having the ability to change their life and, as Myles Munroe put it, provide their "income, input to society, and individual fulfillment." Did you catch that? If you allow it to do so by not treating your gift like a hobby and by developing it like a skill, your gift is the tool that will provide your income, input to society, and individual fulfillment.

If you've ever scrolled through Facebook, talked to another human being, or sat at the lunch table, you may notice that people have a fascination with talking about problems. Though they would hate to admit it, people love complaining about the problems in the world and wishing that all of the problems would disappear. While I do not mean to discredit or downplay the seriousness of many of the issues that surround us, the optimistic side of me feels I have a duty to point out the flaw in this "let's complain about all the problems" mindset that rules the daily lives of so many people around the world.

Complaining about the problems in the world and posting on Facebook about how you wish they would all go away is Latin for "I want to be unemployed." Why? Because in this world, you are paid in accordance to the size of the problems you solve. If you solve small problems like flipping a burger, which I understood is a place where many find themselves, you will get paid a small amount for your services. If you solve big problems, however, like Bill Gates starting Microsoft and revolutionizing the computer industry, the world will reward you accordingly in financial terms. If you want to make money, go work in a mint. If you want to earn money, go solve problems.

The good news, then, is that the world has given you many options and has laid out many problems that need to be solved. The bad news, however, is that many never seem to find success in their attempts to make an impact. They want to do big things but nothing they try ever seems to work while they look over to the next person who seems to have the Midas touch and who seems to prosper in everything they do. They try to open a door and it's locked time and time again, thereby adding to their frustration even more because they know the world is full of problems and options but nothing ever seems to click for them. Why? Because just like a key can't open every door, a person will only find real success in solving problems in the world when they find the door that matches their key. In other words, as mentioned in the previous chapter in the section on finding your project(s), you must find the problem that makes you come alive and that your dominant gift can solve, change, or impact because that is where you are best equipped for success and that is where you will find yourself steady on the path of Purpose Road. Remember, not every project has to be a Mission Impossible, "change the world" type endeavor, but each project will lead you to the next and, if you choose them correctly, will guide you along the path of your purpose day by day.

The common pushback, then, for those who understand they have an incredible ability in this world, no matter their age, race, or background, to discover the gift they were born with and to use that gift to change the world in some way often sounds something like this: "I would launch my project or my dream, but I don't have time because of work or school," or "I want to take time to find and follow my purpose, but I'm stuck in a cycle of all of the immediate responsibilities I have before me, and I can't see myself finding the time in my already busy schedule to make such a discovery and follow such a path." The reality is that millions of people in the world find themselves right now in that very situation, wanting to change their life but feeling stuck and being stuck where they are. If this is you, I want you to pay careful attention to the following anonymous story because this problem you find yourself stuck in is one that will make or break your purpose journey if not addressed because it wouldn't matter if you found out exactly what your purpose was if you also found yourself too stuck where you are to do anything with it.

$86,400

"Imagine there is a bank account that credits your account each morning with $86,400. It carries over no balance from day to day. Every evening the bank deletes whatever part of the balance you failed to use during the day. What would you do? Draw out every cent, of course. Each of us has such a bank. Its name is *time*. Every morning, it credits you with 86,400 seconds. Every night, it writes off as lost whatever of this you have failed to invest to a good purpose. It carries over no balance. It allows no overdraft. Each day, it opens a new account for you. Each night, it burns the remains of the day. If you fail to use the day's deposits, the loss is yours. There is no drawing against tomorrow."

While I understand wholeheartedly that many people who read *The Purpose Playbook* are doing so because they desire a change in their life that centers around their life's purpose but, in the immediate, feel stuck in a cycle of busyness they cannot seem to escape, I am also no stranger to the fact that each of us, whether your name is Oprah Winfrey or whether you're the janitor of the middle school in your town, is allotted 24 hours each day to spend. If you mean to say, then, that you do not have time to find and follow your life's purpose–that which you were born for–then one of two scenarios are likely true. Either an audit of your 24 hours would reveal that you have more time than you think, or sacrifices need to be made in your life to make one of the most important discoveries of your life–finding your life's purpose.

To test if the first is true, think through the previous day of your life minute by minute. How much time did you spend sleeping? How much time did you spending driving or being transported from one place to the next? How much time did you spend at work or at school or at both? How much time did you spend eating? Most of all, how much time did you spend procrastinating or wasting time doing something mindless like scrolling through your phone?

If you are precise and honest about this evaluation, you will likely find that there are hours which exist in your day for you to work on developing your gift and finding your purpose, but every free hour you get, you waste. Don't say you don't have time to work on your purpose if your Netflix history says otherwise. Don't say you don't have time to work on your purpose if your weekends are spent partying. Don't say you don't have time to work on your purpose, if you spend as much time on social media as you do anything else. Mind you, I understand the need to rest, but I also understand how important it is to develop with diligence the gift you have been given and that until you prioritize this development over some of the time you spend resting, you'll rest your way to the grave having never discovered why you lived.

If in evaluating every minute of your day, you discovered that not a single moment was free for you to work on your purpose, you need to make sacrifices because the decision to find your purpose shouldn't be something you negotiate in your head but should be something you decide needs to get done and needs to get done fast. In this season, you may not get your eight hours of sleep each night because you caught an understanding that doing so, which equates to sleeping for 2.3 full 24 hours days each week, may not allow you to put in the time your dream and your gift is going to require.

In this season, you may need to un-signup from some of the commitments you made because, though you care about them, they don't match your purpose. If you work nine to five, what are you doing with the other 16 hours of your day? If you work a job and go to school at the same time, you're going to have to work on your vision in between classes, on lunch breaks, or in the few extra hours you have, but the point is that finding your purpose is what is going to open up your life and bring you the fulfillment you're not getting where you are and the income you're getting from places you were never created to be.

Some reading this right now are in situations, environments, or have workloads that are less conducive to the allotment of "free time" to work on developing their gift and finding their purpose from the perspective of *time*, but if you don't like where you are, nothing is going to change just because you complain about not liking where you are. Nothing is going to change unless you change something. If you want to find your purpose, you must find time to be still. I'm not saying it's easy or the sacrifices you need to make won't be exactly what they sound like– sacrifices. I only mean to say that by finding your purpose, developing your gift, and following the vision for your life, you will do a service to yourself, your family, and your world. I'm not asking you to be fearless in the decision you have to make. I'm asking you to be courageous and to make the decision you know needs to be made right in the face of fear. No one gets to their dreams or purpose solely because of what they are willing to do or because of how busy they are willing to be. Just like packing light for a trip that allows you one bag, people get where they are trying to go because of what they are willing to sacrifice and because of what they are willing to leave behind.

Have you gone all in on the development and usage of your gift, or have you downplayed it and treated it like a hobby? What problem, big or small, will you commit to begin solving, changing, or impacting with your gift as you develop it? What changes and sacrifices in your schedule do you need to make in order to work on your gift and purpose more than you have in the past? Using the lines below, answer the above questions to the best of your ability.

In this short chapter, we zoomed in on the purpose principle of finding your gift and talked about the importance of treating it like something that can change your life and the lives of others instead of a hobby that was just given to you for free time enjoyment. In the next chapter, we will begin to connect the dots we have been making with the principles described thus far and will actually begin crafting your vision step by step so that by the time you finish *The Purpose Playbook*, you will have already begun walking, or even running, on Purpose Road and will have in your hand your custom game plan to do so. Take this next chapter seriously, as it will provide your roadmap with next steps for walking in your unique purpose.

LESSON 6

START YESTERDAY

From the moment in time a person is born that person begins to die. Some die slowly and some die quickly, but the fact remains that our departure from this Earth begins closing in on us the moment we take our first breath until we one day find ourselves in the grave with a tombstone which depicts our name, the year of our birth, the year of our death, and a dash in the middle that represents the time we lived. You didn't choose when you were born, and you won't choose when you pass, but it is in your power to choose what you will do during that dash.

Every single person embarking on this journey called life has come here, whether they know it or not, having been given an assignment, a mission, a purpose that they alone in history possess the ability to fulfill. The problem we face in life, however, is not that we are not gifted enough or equipped enough to complete that assignment which has been given to us but rather that all too often, we run out of time. Why? Because your purpose has a shot clock and that shot clock is the span of time you have been given on this Earth. Far too many people float through life without progressing toward their purpose as if they have all the time in the world to find it, follow it, and fulfill it, and while I understand the importance of pacing yourself on your journey and trusting the process, do understand that *moving* doesn't mean *progressing* any more than having a gym membership means you're in shape.

I have heard people 60+ years old tell me that they don't know their purpose, and if this describes you, know that this book is for you too, but anyone reading these words, young or old, needs to understand that you don't have to get to that place where you look back one day and realize you never discovered what you were created for, but if you are going to avoid this reality, your purpose discovery process must start yesterday. If yesterday has already passed without you beginning your journey, don't be like most people in this world who are always asking when the best time to start is and who make up in their mind that they'll start when they know how everything will play out. Cut your excuses, utilize the playbook in your hand, and start today.

Think for a moment about the GPS on your phone. When you desire to utilize this navigation system, you are doing so because of your understanding that the GPS has the power and the resources to, in a timely manner, get you from where you are to the place you are trying to go. You understand that it holds within it access to the routes and plans that will take you to your destination. You also understand, however, that it will not and cannot give you those plans until you give it the destination. It cannot give you the route or the next steps until you tell it exactly where you are trying to go. In the same way, when it comes to walking out your purpose, you cannot get the next steps without first having a vision of that which you are moving toward.

The first practical step to walking on Purpose Road, the first practical step to changing your life, the first practical step to achieving any major goal you have, the first practical step to living the dream which was deposited in your spirit to bring into the world is to catch a vision of where you are trying to go that is *clear*, *creative*, and *powerful*. In other words, you have to see it before you've got it. You have to know what you're after before you discover how to get it. With that being said, I will now show you how to craft such a vision, how to create a plan for its attainment, and will also give you the opportunity to do so on your own, so that you may begin immediately.

As previously mentioned, the vision you create for your life in alignment with your purpose must be clear, creative, and powerful. These elements must not exist independently but each rely on the presence of the others for the vision to work. Let's take this a step deeper.

1. Your Vision Must Be CLEAR

Anywhere you go on a day to day basis, it is likely you are going to come across a person at some point in time who is wearing glasses. Why? Because poor eyesight is a common problem with common solutions. Whether you're nearsighted or farsighted, struggle seeing at night or all the time, your local eye doctor, trained to fix the problem you face, won't think twice before knowing what he needs to do to help you and will likely show you your options of glasses, contacts, or even laser eye surgeries. Anyone who knows the basics of glasses, however, knows that a person's vision being corrected for the better comes not from merely having a pair of glasses but from having a precise prescription that brings clarity to their unique set of eyes.

In the same way, working to create a vision in your life means very little if it's not clearly and precisely crafted for your unique situation and your unique purpose. Take our GPS, for example. If you try to tell it that you want to go to "a cool place" or "somewhere nice," that GPS can't give you the directions because, though it has so much power, it requires clarity before it can give you access to the power and the potential it has. In the same way, many have great ideas that could change their world, but they will never see those ideas come to life, not because they're incapable of doing so but because they've never taken time to bring clarity to their vision, killing off the ambiguity that paralyzes most of our ideas.

Until you clarify the vision you have, your ideas will forever remain in the idea phase. Perhaps you had an idea to write a book that will never make it to the print phase because "writing a book would be cool" was the extent of your vision. Perhaps that business venture you wanted to start will forever remain an idea because "imagine if I left this deadbeat job and started my own business" was as far as you ever got with your vision of something better for your life. What do you want? What are you after? What is your vision that you would like to see happen? What is your vision for your life? What is your vision for your business? What is your vision for your idea? If you don't bring clarity to the vision, you're bound to become a person who sits around with his or her other "I had a lot of ideas I never acted upon" friends who are bitter and always complain when they see others thrive because they didn't have the guts to clarify their own vision and to bring that vision to life.

To help you understand what I mean on an even more practical level, let's look at a couple examples of a good vision compared to a bad one. As I write these words right now, the date is December 21 and in just over a week, the New Year is going to be among us and millions of people around the world are going to be motivated to start their annual New Year's resolutions that most of them will inevitably keep up for a week or two before giving up on their new vision all together. But why is this the case? While it's not always one single reason that a person quits before fulfilling their vision after the New Year, the reason is often times that the vision they have leaves so much room for ambiguity that the inability to see with clarity the mark they are trying to reach causes a person to quit, and it makes sense.

It's like saying, "This New Year, I want to get in shape" or "I want to lose weight" but because there's no measurable point to aim for, when the New Year's resolution high fades, and you're no longer feeling inspired, you justify in your mind that the one pound you lost constitutes as "losing weight" and so you stop. A better vision would have said something like, "Today is January 1, and by March 31, I commit to losing 20 pounds by working out five times a week and utilizing the new diet and workout plan my trainer sent me." With this as your vision, you can track your progress and will know if you hit the mark or missed it by a specified date because you took the time to make your vision clear.

If all you want to do is lose weight, lose a pound and call yourself a success. If all you want to do is make more money, have your thirty year old self run a lemonade stand, make a few bucks, and have reached your weak, unclear goal. If you want to achieve the larger ones, however, and if you want to make the destiny moves you need to make on Purpose Road before your time runs out, you need to expand your vision and make it very clear. This doesn't mean you won't make adjustments and adaptions along the way, but if you start without a clear vision, I promise you that your "go with the flow" approach to this area of your life will float you anywhere but to the fulfillment of the vision you had.

Another reason it is imperative that your vision be clear is that this clarity gives you the ability to discern what and who should be riding with you in this particular season of your life. If you have no aim or vision of where you're trying to go, having anything or anyone around you won't deter you from your mission because you didn't have a mission in the first place. When you clarify your vision, however, you gain the powerful ability to judge every single decision, opportunity, and person who desires to enter your life by the following question: will this decision, opportunity, or person help me or hurt me as it pertains to arriving at the vision I am moving toward? When you know exactly what that vision is, those decisions become easy. If it's going to hurt the vision, turn it down. If it's going to help the vision, bring it in. If you have a tool to do so, I recommend highlighting or underlining that question and beginning to put it to work in your life right away. You'll be amazed at the power it brings.

With that in mind, think for a moment about your own vision–the place where *you* want to be, not where someone else wants you to be. Perhaps it's one of the purpose projects you wrote in a previous chapter, or perhaps it's a dream or goal you've had for a while but have seen no progress with because no clarity was present. For some of you, your vision looks like one day becoming a doctor, teacher, athlete, business professional, entrepreneur, director, author, or something else. Some of your visions include growing your personal brand and impacting lives in that way, and some of you may have a vision of playing a more behind the scenes, supporting role in the vision of someone else. Regardless, do you know what that place looks like? Do you have a clear vision of where you are trying to go, or are you just going with the flow, hoping that the flow magically takes you to these places? If you want to end up somewhere by choice, today is the day to make clear what that "somewhere" is. In your reach are countless resources you can learn from and countless individuals who are doing what you desire to do and are documenting it for people like yourself to get a glimpse of their world and to achieve similar results if a person is willing to do the work and put in the time it takes to reach those higher levels.

Using the lines provided, I want you to choose one project or endeavor, whether one of your purpose projects or another one you've had, and I want you to craft your vision with as much clarity as possible? Describe what you're trying to do. Describe where you're trying to go. Describe the deadline the vision needs to be attained by. What does this place look like? How do the people in this place carry themselves? Do your research and to the best of your ability, craft a vision that is dangerously clear.

MY CLEAR VISION STATEMENT

____

____

____

____

____

2. Your Vision Must Be CREATIVE

I find it fascinating how many people in life, when it comes to their dreams, goals, and aspirations seem to be looking for a handout as if someone else is obligated to see and to push a vision that was never given them. This could be a gifted individual who discovered their purpose, developed their craft, found their problem, and began to work on their project or vision but stopped when they ceased to see doors open on their behalf. It's not that these individuals necessarily have ill intent but often times is simply that they don't understand how doors of opportunity in life work.

Take, for example, the fact of life that God, as powerful as he is, not once created a door. Instead, he created a tree, and it was up to mankind to use their creativity and imagination to take the wood from the tree and to build a door. In the same way, there are many times in life, as one pursues their vision, that doors will not seem to be present but trees will be all around, and it's because God has blessed mankind with a mind and the ability to think creatively that our possibilities as it pertains to the carrying out of our vision become limitless. While some paths and aspirations, especially those which are more traditional, will provide less room for the creativity I am describing, this reality of the possibilities of creativity is good news for every person who's never fit the mold of the traditional route and desires to tap into their gifts in a more creative fashion, being innovative and unique because their mind is like no one else's in eternity.

Let's say, for example, based on the gifting I have and the problems I feel drawn to impact, I decide to start a business. Let's say specifically that I decided to make a clothing company that specialized in making socks. If with this new venture, my signature design was a plain white sock that was 100% cotton, 100% basic, and had no special features at all, it's more than likely that design would not sell in the market because there's absolutely nothing creative about it at all. It doesn't matter if starting this company was a part of my purpose. If I don't tap into the creativity that God has given me, I do a disservice to every single person I was created to impact because my boring vision ruined my big purpose. If I want run this company successfully, not for the mere sake of fattening my pockets but for the sake of doing that which I was created to do at the level I was supposed to do it, I must tap into the creativity that was given to me.

When Blake Mycoskie and Alejo Nitti, founders of the viral shoe company Toms Shoes, discovered their passion for addressing the problem of kids around the world not having shoes, they didn't just save up some money to buy shoes for a handful of kids or throw up a quick donation page online, making themselves say, "We made an impact." They created a business model that was scalable and allowed them to give away tens of millions of pairs of shoes by using their creativity to decide upon the "buy one pair for yourself, we'll donate one pair to a child in need" model that caught the attention of millions. Do you see the difference? By failing to be creative, they could have helped some but would have missed out on helping tens of millions. Why? Because while a vision adds to your efforts, creativity multiples them.

The problem that many face, however, is that their creativity was knocked out of them when they were young because it was suppressed and looked down upon when really that creativity was supposed to be encouraged and directed so that it could multiply efforts and impact the world. If you feel your creativity has atrophied like the creativity of millions of others, today is the day you must begin to exercise it like a muscle again. If you don't use it, you begin to lose it, but if you begin to work it, you'll see it grow. Start looking at the field you're in and keep an eye out for those creative individuals who challenge the norms and do things differently so you can learn how to do so yourself. While there's no competition for your purpose, it is likely that many have a purpose in a niche or industry where your uniqueness and creativity will be the factors that distinguish you from others. When you find your vision, craft it in such a way that someone else who tries to replicate it couldn't because there's an element of it that's uniquely you–an element you discovered because of your creativity.

In order to tap into this creativity, you first have to know who you're trying to reach with what you're trying to do or create. This means researching the market and finding exactly who your target audience or "dream client" is. You need to find out what they look like, where they congregate, and what problems are unique to them that your gifting and creativity combined can solve, change, or impact. When you know who they are, where they are, and what they need, you then must be creative to figure out how you are going to reach them.

If you make physical products, this could look like setting up a store on Etsy, eBay, or Shopify, starting an Instagram page for the brand, and running targeted ads on Facebook to place your solutions in front of people who have a matching problem, understanding that Facebook is an online home where more than one billion of the world's 7.4 billion people congregate. If your brand is built around providing information or educating people on certain topics, skills, or something of value, you may grow your following with videos on Instagram, YouTube, and especially Facebook because of its powerful sharing feature. When the time comes, you may even use a site like Teachable or Udemy to construct paid video courses for those who want to learn more. In this era, the people are online, so if you're older and still skeptical about the internet, you need to get over that, learn it, and play the game that's being played if you're going to be able to impact lives to the level that's possible.

As you build your vision, be intentional about thinking of or researching creative ways in which social media and the internet can help you manifest the vision you have. Don't start a brand and say, "I'm not making a stupid Facebook page or Instagram account because that stuff is all drama." Get your ego out of the way, eat the meat, and spit out the bone. The world is changing, and it would be a shame to miss what God is trying to do through you today because you're stuck in the ways he used to do things way back when.

Remember, even if you don't call yourself an entrepreneur or businessperson, you are a brand, and you must protect your brand image because damaging it damages the impact you're able to have in the world and ultimately how well you'll be able to walk in your purpose. Whether your route is inherently creative or your route is traditional, you must implement creativity or be passed by the millions who will in the years to come.

Using the lines on the following page and thinking about the vision you recorded in the section on making your vision clear, write out some thoughts on ways you could make your vision more creative, thus more impactful in the world. As I mentioned before, creativity multiplies your efforts, so it's time to get creative. How can your vision be made more creative? How can creativity help you be more intentional about reaching those who need what you have to offer? If they don't know about it, it can't help them, so take this exercise very seriously and find more paper if necessary.

MY VISION'S CREATIVE ELEMENTS

____

____

____

____

____

3. Your Vision Must Be POWERFUL

The third ingredient which cannot be done without as you craft your vision is the need for it to be powerful. A vision that lacks power is a vision that lacks the ability to move you to action, especially in the moments in time where motivation, an unsustainable source of energy, is lacking. Your vision needs to be so powerful that it alone wakes you up in the morning and it alone keeps you up in the later hours of the night. Your vision needs to be so powerful that your motivation becomes intrinsic and working on bringing your vision to life becomes something you're doing when you feel like it and also when you don't. Your vision needs to be so powerful that your thinking switches from the mindset of "I hope this happens" to "this must happen."

Scripture says that when you have a vision, it needs to be written down in a clear manner so that when a person reads it, what is written down will cause them to run. It shouldn't cause them to procrastinate, to crawl, to walk, or to jog. The vision should be so powerful that it causes them to run. Unfortunately, however, as powerful as this principle is, most people in this world have no vision at all, and of those who do have a vision, most of them don't have it written down, and of those few who have a vision that is written down, most of them are not moved by their vision enough to run. Why? Because their vision is weak. Their vision lacks power. If their vision didn't come to pass, it wouldn't bother them at all, so they have no urgency to get it done because it doesn't have to get done.

My vision, which connects to my purpose of helping others find theirs, is written on notecards and is left in places I can see them all the time. When I read them, I'm reminded of why I started this journey in the first place and of all the pain filled eyes I've seen that belonged to hurting people whose voices said the words, "I don't know my purpose." When I look at my vision that's written down on notecards, I'm reminded of the people who take their life every day because they feel they have no purpose. When I look at the vision I crafted, I'm reminded that I wasn't born to complain about the problem. I was sent here to be a part of the solution. For those who are serious about getting serious about their vision, I highly recommend this notecard strategy. Write the vision on the card and keep it close by to read day and night.

You must have a vision that is powerful because its attainment is not up for negotiation. It needs to inspire you and it needs to inspire those individuals God brings to rally around you to help you make it happen. If your vision can be fulfilled without the help of others and especially without God showing up, your vision is far too small compared to your potential that I know is within you.

What part of your vision makes it so powerful that it moves you to action? If your vision didn't come to pass, would you care at all? How can you strengthen your vision statement in a way that causes all who read it to run in its direction? Referring back to your original vision statement then using the lines provided on the following page, write out a new vision statement that incorporates all you have learned in the chapter thus far about the vision ingredients of clarity, creativity, and power. Write something that is dangerously clear, spectacularly creative, and "can't stay the same after reading it" powerful because it reminds you why it must be attained at all costs. This vision will develop over time, but think hard and do the best you can for now.

MY UPDATED CLEAR, CREATIVE, AND POWERFUL VISION STATEMENT

____

____

____

____

____

Once you've crafted this vision, we are led to the next step which stumps many–crafting the plan for the attainment of the vision you have. While many may be able to tell you what they desire or even what their vision is, the bigger question remains: what is the plan to make that vision, dream, or idea become a reality? How are you going to pull it off? In the words of Chris Gardner, whose story inspired the movie *The Pursuit of Happyness*, your plan needs to be "clear, concise, compelling, committed, and consistent to achieve any sort of success." Most people make plans containing few of these elements, if any, and the result is that they seldom "achieve any sort of success," but this is not going to be the case with you. Why? Because your plan is going to contain these elements.

Back to our example of the GPS, the navigation system will never give you the route until the vision is clear. In the same way, as you spend time praying over the vision you have crafted and submitting it back to God to purify it, the plan is going to come but not until the vision is clear. Using the clear, creative, and powerful vision you crafted, however, you can now insert it into the destination section of God's Positioning System and the plans will come, but you have to first understand how God's plans work. In scripture, the Psalmist tells us that God's Word is "a light unto our path and a lamp unto our feet." As you navigate Purpose Road and you seek to fulfill your visions in life, God's direction is often going to look like a lamp unto your feet in which you don't see the whole journey but rather, just like a GPS giving you the next turn to make, you are just given the next step.

The key is to know where you are, to know where you are trying to go, and to be faithful in the process by doing what needs to be done today to progress you down the path. Sometimes you're going to mess up, and sometimes you're going to make the wrong turn, but just like a GPS recalibrates and gives you a new route, making the wrong turn doesn't mean you fail and the journey is over. It only means that adjustments need to be made and that your journey to your purpose and vision will come about by a different route than you previously intended or with a different estimated time of arrival than you expected.

On a practical level, developing your vision's plan looks, first, like setting aside the time in your schedule to actually do so and also to have a mind that is always available to receive inspired ideas and last minute detours that could better your success. When a better idea or plan comes out of nowhere, don't be so prideful or emotionally attached to your bad idea or lesser idea that you let it destroy your vision. So, find a space where you can find separation from the noise and distractions that are filling your mind each day. If music in the background turns on the creative side of your mind, then feel free to have it playing.

Second, on a sheet of paper or in the notes section of your phone, I want you to make a numbered list that takes up twenty lines, and in this brainstorming exercise, I want you to record twenty ideas, some basic and some creative, some in your reach and some out of your reach, that could progress you toward making your vision a reality. Start with this amount for now, and add to the list as more ideas come.

For example, if your vision involves starting a clothing line that promotes some sort of message that you are passionate about, your twenty item list may include a few of the following: creating an Instagram page, designing the first collection of merchandise, contacting influencers in the niche who may promote your brand in exchange for free items, building a website to sell your products on, connecting with someone who has done what you are trying to do and asking them questions about what to do and what to avoid, etc. Again, use your list to brainstorm small steps, large steps, and everything in between while asking God to send inspiration, ideas, and steps you would have missed. Keep this list with you and be ready to write in it as new ideas come throughout the day, for it's sad to think of the amount of ideas each of us receive on a daily basis but don't record or simply do nothing with. Some of your ideas will be great and some will never be used, but recording them gives you an opportunity that most people miss out on because they forget what they failed to record.

With this ideas list readily available, the next step in crafting your plan is to create a new list on paper or on your phone that is numbered one through six. This task is the most important in progressing efficiently toward the fulfillment of your vision. Unlike the first list which collects your ideas to pull from and is added to indefinitely as those ideas come, this six item list is for today and today only. On this six item list, you will record the top six tasks which need to get done on that particular day that directly correlate toward progressing you toward the vision you wrote down.

For example, back to our clothing line illustration, today's six tasks may include: 1. Start the Instagram account, 2. Purchase the domain name, 3. Create the website, 4. Confirm and finalize pricing and shipping costs, 5. Schedule a photoshoot, and 6. Confirm the release date. Notice, all six items on this list are in your power to complete today but could have easily fallen prey to procrastination because we grow distracted by so many trivial tasks throughout the day that we often don't get the most important ones done. If, however, you complete these six tasks in one day, you will have already done what most people would drag out over the course of a week or more. After you complete them, you will see the progress you've made toward your vision, will be inspired because of the size of the tasks you completed, and will catch a wave of momentum that you can ride to the next day's six tasks. This wave was only made possible because you knew where you wanted to be in the future and focused on the critical tasks not of a month from now but of today.

Focus each day to complete all six, but if one of them is left undone, leave it on the list for the next day. Be sure that you also check on your running idea list on a regular basis to see which of those ideas can be transformed into tasks that you can add to your six item list on the appropriate day. Please be sure to note as well that the daily list is not about the mere satisfaction of crossing things off that may lead to some placing baby sized tasks on their list like "brush my teeth so I feel ready for the day." The list is also not about adding ten to twenty items.

The purpose of the list is to cause you to focus only on the most important, critical tasks that would otherwise face the risk of being attacked by the assassin of procrastination. This process works for the individual's personal vision as much as it does the company and their quarterly goals, for it is *time* that often robs us all in the wasted hours, minutes, and seconds of our days that we can never get back.

Using the lines provided and revisiting the updated vision statement you recorded on an earlier page, fill in your first six item daily list and begin putting it into action immediately. The best day to start was yesterday, but if you didn't start yesterday, the best day to start is today. For those who are especially serious about their vision being fulfilled, I challenge you to make finding an accountability partner for the fulfillment of your vision one of the first tasks on your list because as we talked about earlier, accountability will boost your efficiency.

MY DAILY TASK LIST

1. ________________________________
2. ________________________________
3. ________________________________
4. ________________________________
5. ________________________________
6. ________________________________

Make a practice of implementing these six tasks every single day, focusing on remaining "clear, concise, compelling, committed, and consistent." On the journey toward your purpose and the visions you have for the many projects you will begin during your lifetime on Purpose Road, God will shape you, guide you, and provide you with whispers of ideas, inspiration, and new plans along the way. The more consistent you are in today's tasks, the more faith you'll build for the tasks of tomorrow. Stretch yourself, get out of your comfort zone, and trust the process day by day, for two things are certain: this world needs what you have to offer and God blesses consistency.

LESSON 7

BURN THE FREAKING BOATS

The year was 1519 when Hernán Cortés and about 600 of his Spanish soldiers set out for mission possible when they traveled to conquer the powerful Aztec empire who possessed gold and riches men could only dream of and who, for the last 600 years, had defeated every powerful army that sought to conquer them. Cortés was not naive to this information, nor was he naive to the fact that it didn't look as if his 600 soldiers really stood a chance. Besides, armies of the past were much more equipped than his men and still failed to defeat the Aztecs. Cortés' strategy, however, was different than that of those who failed. As his 600 soldiers marched toward the enemy, Cortés proclaimed three powerful words–"BURN THE BOATS." He made it clear to his men that they would either conquer the enemy or die trying. He made it clear that if they were going to make it home, it would be on the boats of the enemy. With no other options, Cortés and his 600 men, ill-equipped for a battle of this caliber, fought with everything they had and became the first army in 600 years to succeed in this daunting task of conquering the Aztecs, not because they were a stronger army than the enemy but because they burned the boats.

THE COST OF BOATS UNBURNED

Hundreds of years later, it is likely that the task before you does not involve burning physical boats or using physical weapons to fight for your life, but what I do know to be true is that each of us have the opportunity to settle for what has always been done in our life, our family, our neighborhood, our city, etc., and we also have the opportunity to decide that we will choose another route that may not be as crystal clear as the status quo but provides us the chance to bet on ourselves and to bet on the call of God on our lives, walking in our purpose and changing the world as we know it.

I understand that, at this present moment, not everyone has the faith to make such a leap away from all that seems secure and toward their purpose, but I also understand that just as there is a cost to burning the boats, there is an even greater cost to leaving the boats unburned.

When you leave the boats unburned, you rob every single person in history of that which you were born to bring into the world. When you leave the boats unburned, you set yourself up to one day die without ever having discovered why you lived and having never experienced all that you were supposed experience and having never felt that feeling that comes from doing something with your life that you can confidently say you were put on this Earth to do. When you leave the boats unburned, you may look like a success, but you fail in life for deciding not to follow your life's purpose, and every single day, you will feel that sting deep down in your soul that comes from not knowing why you're here, or worse, not running after it when it's known.

It's tragic that our society for so long has operated as a machine that disregards the idea of purpose all together but instead is created to feed people into the system to work a job that's "better than nothing" for 40+ years before retiring with a nice watch and that being all there is, but the fact that the system is in place doesn't make it accurate. The fact that the school system has become our benchmark for measuring how successful a kid will become does not make it accurate. The fact that millions, dare I say billions, of people in this world have zero idea why they, as an individual, are here does not mean that is the way it's supposed to be.

Finding and following your purpose is more than possible. It's attainable. But doing so is the result of more than reading *The Purpose Playbook* and learning how to find and follow your purpose. You have the keys, you have the tools, you have the knowledge, but only you can burn the boats. Only you can decide in your own life, whether you're a 19 year old college student or a 49 year old working single mother with two kids, if you will burn the boats that need to be burned in order to get where you have to get and do what you were created to do.

Burning the boats doesn't look like burning some boats while leaving one or two just in case the mission doesn't work out or you change your mind. If you give 90% of your effort to Plan A but hold out on the last 10% because it was reserved for Plan B, don't point fingers at anybody when you miss the mark by that last 10%. If you want Plan A–your purpose–to work out, you have to go all in. You have to go all in with your conviction. You have to go all in with your gift. You have to go all in with the problem you have chosen to attack. And you have to go all in with the projects you pursue on Purpose Road.

If you've been gifted with an amazing voice to sing that you won't make public because you don't "think of yourself as a singer," stop hiding and stop robbing the kid who, while at a low point in his or her life, is going to stumble across a song you wrote that depicts how you overcame a low point in your life, and that song will, or was supposed to, save the kid's life. If you've been given a story or words to write but, like I did for so many years, you always talk about writing a book one day, or perhaps you started writing a book one or two years ago that you never finished, go on a trip by yourself, bring your laptop or notebook, and write your story.

It's going to change your life because you'll learn the power of finishing what you start, you'll be liberated from something that once remained only in your head, and your words that were given to you to write are going to inspire others to find and follow their purpose as well. The purpose business is not about addition. We're in the business of multiplication, for as we follow our purpose instead of following the world and its systems, cycles, and flows which we accept as truth without even thinking, we liberate others as well, and we change their life.

In her world famous poem, *Our Deepest Fear*, Marianne Williamson writes the famous words, "Our deepest fear is not that we are inadequate. Our deepest fear is that we are powerful beyond measure. It is our light, not our darkness that most frightens us. We ask ourselves, 'Who am I to be brilliant, gorgeous, talented, fabulous?' Actually, who are you not to be? You are a child of God. Your playing small does not serve the world. There's nothing enlightened about shrinking so that other people won't feel insecure around you. We are all meant to shine, as children do. We were born to make manifest the glory of God that is within us. It's not just in some of us; it's in everyone. And as we let our own light shine, we unconsciously give other people permission to do the same. As we're liberated from our own fear, our presence automatically liberates others." Somebody is waiting for you to burn the boats. Somebody needs you to find and follow your life's purpose.

What boats in your life are standing in the way of your purpose that need to be burned once and for all so that you can become all that you were created to be? Perhaps it's a relationship or friendship with someone whose negative words keep you from following your dream. Perhaps it's an excuse, fear, thought, or idea about yourself or your ability that isn't even true but that you keep replaying in your mind to talk yourself out of embarking on a new journey for your life. Whatever you've been resorting to that is holding you back from finding and following your purpose is a boat that needs to be burned if you will have any chance of doing so. Using the lines below, write out the boats in your life that need to be burned, and write your initials next to each one if you are committed to burning them.

THE BOATS I NEED TO BURN

____

____

____

____

____

BET ON YOURSELF

As I said at the beginning of this book, "the wisdom I share may not match your grandma's keys to success, but perhaps those keys can't open the doors you need to open in this era and the era to come." When you catch the vision for your life's purpose that you know in your soul is for you, is calling you, and refuses to be silent, you have the opportunity to pretend as though you don't hear it in an effort to please those around you–your parents, your guidance counselors, or others who may want you to play this life safe–or you can answer the call and bet on yourself because you know what you've got to offer, and you understand that when those people are gone, you are going to be left with your life, even if it's not the one you wanted. It's not easy but it's simple. No one is going to make you follow your purpose and, in fact, many will try to steer you from it, but God has given you the power of decision, and it's not what we want that changes our lives. It's what we decide, commit to, and execute on. Find your purpose, stick to the plan, and manifest a life most will never be able to conceive because they didn't have the guts to burn the boats, bet on themselves, and walk in their life's purpose.

EXECUTION

It is an unfortunate reality that most people in this world will die without ever discovering why they lived. Most people will die without ever taking a step on Purpose Road and without ever tapping into their gifts or potential. This is not to say that the people described were without dreams, aspirations, visions, ideas, or even plans. It is only to say that most of these people lacked execution. Most of these people were turned away for one reason or another and never started or never finished the projects which were placed in their heart to work on during their time on this Earth.

It was Martin Luther King Jr. who said, “If you can't fly then run, if you can't run then walk, if you can't walk then crawl, but whatever you do you have to keep moving forward,” and I tell you today, about the purposes and dreams that are in your heart, they are possible. Let no one convince you otherwise. There will be days when you make leaps and bounds and other days when you lack the motivation to get out of bed, but making dreams come true was never about what you feel like doing. It has always been about doing what needs to be done. Making dreams come true was never about motivation. It has always and will always be about discipline. No matter the day, no matter your mood, the world needs you to keep moving forward.

With all of that in mind, it is inevitable that there will be two types of responses from those who have found their way to the final pages of *The Purpose Playbook.* First, there will be those who connected with the words they read and, at the very least, caught an understanding that there is more to their life than what they're living and will make a pursuit toward finding and following their purpose from this day forward. Secondly, however, there will be those who read the pages, either acknowledged or failed to acknowledge how serious the purpose problem is, but still will put the book down and will return back to a life they know does not match what they were created for but that they've decided to make a home in.

Only you can decide which group will describe you, and for those who are deciding to find and follow their life's purpose, I want you to know that this is a purpose movement, this is a purpose family, and we're in it together, running after the call of God on our lives. And for those who made the decision to read the pages of this book but do nothing about their purpose at all, I still have hope because even if you reject the idea that there's a purpose for your life that you're yet to discover, the pull of purpose this book has casted out has connected with your soul and will call you until you answer from now until forever, for "the mind of man, once stretched by a new idea or experience, never returns back to its original dimensions" (Oliver Wendell Holmes).

ONE LAST SECRET

Not long ago, while I was speaking on the phone with a friend of mine who happens to be very successful in his business ventures and projects, I asked him to give me the best advice he could offer, and he gave me two words that I want to give to you–"FAIL FAST." Not everything you try to do in pursuit of your purpose is going to be a smashing success, but when something doesn't work, fail fast, get up fast, and get on to the next thing. Your failures mold you, shape you, and teach you in preparation for the success you are to see in your future, but if you give up the first time something doesn't work out, you will see no success in your life no matter how gifted you are or how big your purpose is. This is all a marathon, not a sprint, so take time to learn from every mistake and every failure because you'll one day look back and see that the failures were the biggest blessings in disguise. Practice persistence, bet on yourself, bet on your God, and you will find and follow your life's purpose before your clock runs out.

PURPOSE MERCH!

PURPOSEGANGWORLDWIDE.CO

THE PURPOSE COLLECTION

GET 10% OFF WITH
CODE: P2PLAYBOOK

"BY PURCHASING ONE OF OUR EXCLUSIVE PURPOSE TEES OR HOODIES, YOU'RE JOINING THE FIGHT TO TAKE HOPE AND PURPOSE TO THE WORLD."
KYLE DENDY

BOOKING

KYLEDENDY.COM/BOOKING

THE PURPOSE TOUR

Do you need a speaker who will shift the atmosphere of all who attend?

Bring Kyle and *The Purpose Playbook* to your next corporate, church, or school event.

Share How the Book Impacted Your Life:

KyleDendy.com/stories

Connect With Kyle:

Instagram.com/KyleDendy

Facebook.com/KyleDendy

Twitter.com/KyleDendy

YouTube.com/KyleDendy

Purpose Apparel:

PurposeGangWorldwide.co

Instagram.com/PurposeGangWorldwide

84277674R00121

Made in the USA
Lexington, KY
21 March 2018